Learner-Directed Assessment in ESL

Learner-Directed Assessment in ESL

Edited by

Glayol Ekbatani
St. John's University

Herbert Pierson
St. John's University

LAWRENCE ERLBAUM ASSOCIATES, PUBLISHERS

2000   Mahwah, New Jersey   London

Lawrence Erlbaum Associates, Inc., Publishers
10 Industrial Avenue
Mahwah, NJ 07430

Cover design by Kathryn Houghtaling Lacey

Library of Congress Cataloging-in-Publication Data

Learner-directed assessment in ESL / editors: Glayol Ekbatani, Herbert Pierson.
    p. cm.
    Includes bibliographical references and index.
ISBN 0-8058-3067-7 (alk. paper). — ISBN 0-8058-3068-5
    (pbk : alk. paper)
1. English language—Study and teaching—Foreign speakers.
    2. English language—Ability testing. I. Ekbatani, Glayol.
    II. Pierson, Herbert D. (Herbert DeLeon), 1941–
PE1128.A2L359   1999
428'.007 —dc21   99-17875
                                                      CIP

Printed in the United States of America
10 9 8 7 6 5 4 3 2 1

For my parents, Parvin and Saed, and my beloved aunt, Afagh
Glayol Ekbatani

For Angela, David, and Rebecca
Herbert Pierson

Contents

Foreword

Lyle F. Bachman
University of California, Los Angeles

Two recent movements in applied linguistics—learner-centered language teaching and a renewed interest in the authenticity, interactiveness, and impact of language assessments—have come together to bring about a greater concern for and interest in expanding the role of the learner or test-taker in the assessment process. Learner-centered teaching has focused not only on the types of learning activities or tasks with which learners interact in language classes, but also on greater involvement of learners in directing their own learning. Interest in facilitating self-directed learning has led to the development of self-access or independent learning centers, where learners work by themselves, in pairs, and in small groups, interacting in a wide variety of activities involving a vast array of technologies, from tape and video players to live satellite transmissions to the most sophisticated computer-based multimedia learning programs, as well as human tutors and group facilitators. What has often been slighted in both learner-centered classroom activities and self-access centers is the development of appropriate assessment procedures in which learners are not only test-takers but also active participants in the assessment process. The chapters in this volume provide some useful insights into this issue and suggest a number of approaches for greater involvement of learners in the assessment process. Interest among language testers in making language assessments more authentic and interactive, and for facilitating positive impact on test-takers, has led to renewed interest in assessment procedures such as self-assessment and portfolios, and research into the application of research tools such as verbal self-reports and the analysis of self-repairs to the purposes of assessment.

These shared interests among language teachers and language testers have led to the development of an exciting range of approaches to assessment, many of which are discussed here. These approaches share two common interests: (a) developing assessment tasks and procedures that are more closely related to learning and teaching tasks, and (b) involving learners in the assessment process (i.e., in designing or selecting their own learning or assessment tasks and procedures, and in assessing themselves). There are also several common assessment issues that these approaches need to address: (a) the purpose of the assessment, (b) the content to be assessed, (c) the types of assessment tasks or procedures to be used, (d) the appropriate procedures for administering the assessments, and (e) the appropriate method for assessing performance and providing feedback to learners and other test-users.

The most important consideration in any assessment is the purpose, or use, for which it is intended, so that it is essential for developers of learner-directed assessments to clearly specify the purpose for which these are intended. Assessments can be used for a variety of purposes, including appropriate placement; self-access activity; diagnostic feedback to the learner; and the formative evaluation of learning materials, content, activities, and delivery system. Formative assessment purposes such as these lend themselves most easily to greater learner involvement. The challenge will be to appropriately involve learners in assessment for summative purposes, such as admission to a program, certification of achievement, or to demonstrate accountability to institutions.

The content of the assessment tasks or the areas of language ability to be assessed also needs to be clearly specified. This can be based on material covered in a course syllabus, on a learner's own self-directed learning plan, or on independent material or objectives outside of the course or learning activities themselves. In addition to assessing areas of language ability, it may be useful to assess other qualities of learners, such as their affective responses to learning or self-access activities, the various strategies they may employ in these, and the relative effectiveness of the learner's own involvement in both the learning and the assessment process. The challenge here, I believe, will be to develop creative approaches to assessing qualities of learners, such as affective responses and strategy use, that may be relatively difficult to access.

The types of assessment tasks to be included can vary in so many ways that careful consideration needs to be given to the potential authenticity and interactiveness of these tasks. Following Bachman and Palmer's (1996) definition, *authenticity* pertains to the extent to which the characteristics of assessment tasks correspond to the characteristics of tasks in a specific target language use (TLU) domain, either that of the language classroom or self-access materials, or that of a particular real-life domain in which learners will eventually use the language they are learning. Bachman and Palmer (1996) defined *interactiveness* as to the extent to which the abilities or attributes that we want to assess are engaged, or elicited, by the assessment task. Tasks that are highly interactive and perceived as relatively authentic by test-takers are likely to engage them in language use and to provide language samples on which can be based valid inferences about the abilities to be assessed. One challenge will be to clearly identify and describe, collaboratively with learners, the language-use tasks in the appropriate TLU domain. Another challenge will be to apply the same creativity and ingenuity to designing and developing assessment tasks, also in collaboration with learners, as goes into the design of learning tasks, so that assessment tasks correspond to TLU tasks, and engage the abilities we want to assess.

Learner-directed assessment tasks can also be administered in a variety of ways, either as part of the learning materials and activities themselves, or as separate activities, either individually or in a group, and by a person or a machine. In classroom settings, for example, assessment activities can be built in at the end of lessons or units of learning, whereas in a computer-assisted language-learning setting, the learning program can be written to provide a record-keeping function, tracking not only learner responses, but also the different learning tasks that are attempted. An equally viable alternative is to provide a separate set of assessment tasks and activities that learners engage in at appropriate times, as determined by either the progress of the class or the stages in an independent learning plan through which the learner passes. In either case, the challenge will be to implement an assessment schedule that will be flexible enough to fit learners' individual developmental stages in learning while also meeting standards of comparability and equity of assessment.

The final issues to be considered pertain to how to assess or score performance on assessment tasks and how to report this in the most useful way for both test-users and test-takers. One consideration is to decide who assesses the performance. Although this is typically done by individuals such as teachers, administrators, self-access monitors, or tutors, rather than the test-takers, an important consideration in learner-directed assessment is how, and under what conditions, the learner can most appropriately be involved in the actual assessment. Self-assessment provides an approach in which learners typically rate themselves according to a number of criteria or dimensions. Portfolios provide an approach in which learners typically provide verbal descriptions and narratives evaluating their work. Irrespective of who does the assessment, this can be done in essentially three ways:

1. A score based on the sum of a number of responses (e.g., a questionnaire or a set of "can-do" statements to which the learner answers *yes* or *no*, with the score being the number of *yes* responses).

2. A score or scores based on some sort of rating scale (e.g., either a single holistic rating scale of language ability, or a set of analytic rating scales for different aspects of the ability to be assessed, on which learners rate themselves on a numerical scale as high, middle, or low).

3. A verbal description of performance (e.g., a verbal description of a number of tasks that were performed, along with a description of the learner's performance on these tasks).

Deciding which performance assessment procedure, or some combination thereof, should be used depends on how the abilities to be assessed and the purposes for which the assessment is intended have been specified. When the assessment is done by individuals other than the test-takers, it is important that feedback be as rich and meaningful as possible. This may entail different reporting formats for different test-users, such as test-takers, teachers, administrators, parents, and funding agencies. When the assessment is done by the test-takers, either by themselves or in collaboration with others, knowledge of their own performance and of the assessment criteria and process in itself provides meaningful feedback and can enhance self-awareness. Whatever the approach to assessing performance used in learner-directed assessment, the challenge will be finding a means for including and representing the perspective and discourse of the learners or test-takers themselves, while meeting standards of reliability and accountability.

In conclusion, learner-directed assessment provides a meeting place for much of the current thinking about language learning, teaching, and assessment, and constitutes an exciting direction for inquiry, research, and development, as witnessed by the chapters in this volume. At the same time, it presents a number of challenges, and the ways in which we meet these challenges will undoubtedly provide valuable insights into the nature of language learning, language teaching, and language assessment.

Preface

Learner-Directed Assessment in ESL is a theme-based book that examines the relationship between the language learner and actual language assessment processes. The book promotes assessment approaches that involve the ordinary learner in the testing process and provides insight in learner-directed methods that investigate and enhance the validity and reliability of current assessment instruments. The motivation for writing this book has come from recent progress that supports the learner-directed language classroom. The contributors to this book are linked together by their shared determination to move learner-directed assessment forward as a cornerstone of the learner-centered classroom.

The chapters in this book are grounded in current pedagogical applications of authentic assessment measures and are principally targeted at busy classroom teachers and program directors who are seeking ways to include their students in the evaluation process. Professional language testers in search of authenticity in assessment and desiring to create more interactive evaluation tools would likewise derive benefit from the chapters in this book.

It is the editors' hope that this book will be a modest contribution to the assessment field because of the attention it gives to the issues of reliability and validity in learner-directed assessment. Although the benefits of learner-directed assessment might be accepted by teachers, incorporating more authentic assessment tools in the classroom is often frustrated by the issues of validity and reliability. The book attempts to be a meeting place where teachers and assessment specialists can consider these issues at a deeper level.

ACKNOWLEDGMENTS

Finally, we would like to acknowledge the help of a former colleague and teacher, Lyle Bachman, whose kind words and professional advice spurred us on in this endeavor. Also, we would like to thank Fr. David O'Connell, the former Dean of St. John's College of Arts and Science, now President of the Catholic University of America, for his unwavering institutional support; Naomi Silverman, Lori Hawver, and Barbara Wieghaus, editors at Lawrence Erlbaum Associates, for their patience and encouragement; and Bob Barone, Louise McKenzie, and Jeff Melnik of the Professional Development and Training Center at St. John's University for their superb advice in producing the final manuscript.

—*Glayol Ekbatani*
—*Herbert Pierson*

Chapter 1

Moving Toward Learner-Directed Assessment

Glayol Ekbatani
St. John's University

As the implementation of the learner-centered English as a Second Language (ESL) curriculum remains a primary goal for the majority of ESL training institutions and in the ESL classroom itself (Nunan, 1988), many practitioners and assessment specialists have, in recent years, sought ways to encourage the active involvement of learners in the process of language assessment. Nunan (1988) argued that "in a learner-centered curriculum model both teachers and learners need to be involved in evaluation" (p. 116). Dickinson (1987) reported on the importance of the student's involvement in assessment in a student-centered curriculum. Presenting a detailed chart on various phases of self-instruction, he illustrated how successful learner-centered instruction entails learners undertaking responsibility for their learning, and how achievement of responsibility for learning entails learners' involvement in assessment. Le Blanc and Painchaud (1985) stated that "being part of the completed learning cycle should imply being involved in the assessment process, since evaluation is now recognized as a component in the educational process" (p. 73). Similar in scope to the leaner-centered curriculum, learner-directed assessment (a) provides the learner with the necessary tools and guidance for self-assessment, (b) investigates the strategies test-takers use in responding to test questions, and most importantly, (c) relies on a process-oriented approach to assessment rather than a single testing instrument.

Nevertheless, despite the considerable emphasis placed on student inclusion in the process of assessment, test development in most educational

1

fields is still, to some extent, the domain of teachers and testing organizations with little or no input from the learner. Heron (1981) observed that the prevailing model for assessing student work in higher education is an authoritarian one. Staff exercise unilateral intellectual authority. Students do not significantly participate in decision making about their learning objectives or learning programs, or in setting criteria and applying them in assessment procedures. As revealed in the studies reported in this volume, such exclusion of language learners in the crucial process of test development has led to significant discrepancies in the respondents' test scores and their actual communicative abilities. Thus, our limited knowledge of the learners' test-taking strategies has raised major questions about the validity of standardized norm-referenced tests as solid predictors of language skills. Moreover, there have been few books or monographs offering tangible and concrete guidance for practitioners who strive to empower their students in becoming active partners in the overall evaluation process.

This volume was written to meet some of these challenges. An important theme that emerges from the chapters in this book is that the active inclusion of the language learner in the testing process is a necessary step in moving toward autonomy in language acquisition, gaining more insight to improve the reliability and validity of testing instruments, heightening learner awareness of personal strengths and challenges, and stressing the pedagogical nature of language assessment. This volume looks at the relationship between the learner and actual language-assessment processes.

SELF-ASSESSMENT

Self-assessment, which is presented here by North (chap. 2) and Strong-Krause (chap. 3), has been investigated by a number of researchers as a powerful learner-directed assessment tool that heightens learner awareness of personal strengths and weaknesses, and promotes language acquisition. As already mentioned, Nunan (1988) argued that learner self-assessment can be an important supplement to teacher assessment and that self-assessment provides one of the most effective means of developing both critical self-awareness of what it is to be a learner and skills to learn how to learn. In stating his reasons for recommending self-assessment, Dickinson (1987) suggested the following: (a) assessment leading toward evaluation is an important objective in its own right and training learners in this is beneficial to learning; (b) assessment is a necessary part of self-direction; and (c) in self-instructional programs involving many students, the assessment demands made by the students are very heavy, and self-assessment is one way of alleviating the teacher's assessment burden.

Although few people dispute the value of self-assessment as one of the cornerstones of autonomous learning, concerns have been expressed on the validity of self-assessment techniques used as a basis for making decisions such as selection, grading, and certification. According to Dickinson (1992), self-assessment may not be an adequate tool when evaluation is undertaken for the purpose of awarding recognition of achievement or withholding that recognition from a candidate. Concerns have been raised about learners' objectivity and capacity to view their attainments. However, Dickinson (1992) reported that there is considerable scope for self-assessment when tests designed for assessing proficiency are used as a learner–teacher feedback device. He stated:

> Much assessment that goes on in the classroom is primarily concerned with the learning process, indicating to learners the degree to which they have achieved a standard of performance which is adequate for a particular situation. This is formative assessment and it is with formative assessment that self-assessment largely belongs. (p. 33)

To broaden the scope of formative assessment, Le Blanc and Painchaud (1985) included placement among the functions of self-assessment. Their study convincingly demonstrated that guided self-assessment could be considered a valuable tool for placement. Furthermore, it has been noted that given adequate knowledge of the purpose of placement exams and their role in determining the level of instruction, language learners see no advantage in falsifying a self-estimated report on their abilities. They are often as concerned as the examiners about receiving accurate placements. In this volume, Strong-Krause examines the use of self-assessment as a placement instrument.

Le Blanc and Painchaud (1985) also identified two additional factors that contribute to the effective implementation of self-assessment, namely, creating (a) concrete linguistic situations where the learners can self-assess their communicative ability, and (b) good descriptors that will in turn produce good predictive items. North's chapter focuses on these factors, the development of concrete task-based descriptors, a major breakthrough in the current study of self-assessment.

North first considers the current research he has undertaken in Switzerland to develop empirically verifiable proficiency scales that define different aspects of language use at different levels, and how these scales and descriptors can serve as valuable tools for ESL professionals, especially curriculum planners. North's data analysis has so far produced a defined 10-band scale of language proficiency and a bank of classified, calibrated descriptors covering a relatively large number of categories. In addition, he reports on his progress in developing prototype self-assessment and teacher-assessment instruments as a means to produce individual language portfolios that record the learner's achievement in relation to a common scale of language proficiency.

North was originally motivated to undertake this project because of the growing concern raised among practitioners about the validity and reliability of existing proficiency scales, many of which are produced mainly by single authors or small committees. The scales of language proficiency and the bank of calibrated descriptors mentioned in this chapter are based on a descriptive scheme that draws on models of competence and proficiency (Canale & Swaine, 1980), and the Rasch Item Response Theory measurement model (Jones, 1993), using a variant that takes account of assessor subjectivity to judge learner proficiency. Additionally, North draws extensively on feedback from a linguistic checklist prepared by teachers of English and other languages.

The contribution to assessment research reported in North's chapter is twofold. First, he enhances the reliability and validity of authentic assessment instruments, such as tests of spoken production, through empirically developed proficiency scales and the creation of brief, clear, and independent descriptors. Second, he engages the learner in self-assessment tasks, while using these clear and defined descriptors. In addition, North demonstrates how his research aims at involving the learner in developing a language portfolio containing a personalized self-assessment checklist that describes what they think they can or cannot do as well as a report on their exam results and language-learning achievements. The personalized language portfolio that is the product of this effort can be submitted to authorities for the purpose of seeking employment or admission to an academic institution. Thus, not only are learners empowered to assess their language proficiency, but they are also able to show and display their real language-learning achievements.

He also studies the use of self-assessment ratings as part of the placement procedure. Although reports on the degree of correlation of self-assessment and traditional tests are varied, there seems to be a general consensus that more specific self-assessment tasks have shown a higher correlation with objective measures of testing language proficiency.

In her chapter, Strong-Krause examines the degree of specificity of the self-assessment tasks that are needed to obtain accurate results. She also examines the types of tasks that best predict placement in ESL programs, presenting three categories of self-assessment—global, specific context, and actual. After a thorough statistical analysis of the data using stepwise regression analysis, Strong-Krause concludes that the task that best correlates with the traditional placement test is when respondents rate themselves on a detailed description of a given task. She also found that of the four skill areas surveyed, learner assessment of speaking ability was the best predictor, accounting for almost half of the variance in placement test scores.

The data presented in this chapter is of special value to Intensive English Program (IEP) directors, especially when self-assessment is used in conjunction with traditional placement exams. First, it adds to the validity of the objective multiple choice exams because it has direct representation from the learner. Second, it addresses one of the major problems that many program directors face in reviewing overseas applicants whose level of English proficiency can only be determined after they arrive. A lack of knowledge of the language ability of prospective students makes almost impossible the already difficult task of advance planning. This problem affects small programs that may not be able to offer all the levels on a regular basis unless there are adequate numbers in each level. Currently, the only indicator of the overseas applicants' language proficiency are scores on standardized tests, yet the high cost and the long turn around period of such tests might discourage students from choosing the programs that require such scores. Thus, self-assessment could serve a viable source of information in such cases. In the final section of her chapter, Strong-Krause presents guidelines for the development of self-assessment instruments. The self-assessment questionnaires developed in her study and included in the appendix could be easily implemented in most IEP programs.

SELF-REPAIR

In the previous section, the role of self-assessment as a necessary part of self-directed learning and assessment was discussed. Self-repair, in chapter 4 written by Erna Van Hest, is yet another area where self-assessment has a major place. Self-assessment directed toward self-repair allows language learners to judge their performance in short stretches of discourse and make changes on their own initiative when they find deviations from the standard norms.

Under appropriate guidance, self-repair can be an effective communication strategy that leads learners to more proficiency. Moreover, the self-repair behavior of learners or what gets repaired at different stages can be used as a measure of L2 (second-language) proficiency. This chapter presents self-repair in its role as an alternative to language assessment.

In her chapter, Van Hest demonstrates how the examination of spontaneous learner self-corrections can be helpful input for classroom language assessment. With great detail, she introduces the phenomenon of self-repair by discussing the task of self-repair identification and classification and by presenting examples of self-repair data. These she categorizes as phonological, morphological, lexical, syntactic, and level of appropriateness.

Van Hest describes self-repair as the corrections learners make on their own initiative. Self-repair behavior indicates the workings of the speech monitor. To illustrate this, Van Hest presents a model of how self-repair data is identified and classified. In this model, she calls the original utterance the *reparandum*. This is followed immediately by an editing process where the original utterance is interrupted and corrected. The corrected result is called the *reparatum*.

Van Hest shows how self-assessment is related to language assessment by reporting the results of her 4-year research project on the L1 (first-language) and L2 self-repair behavior of Dutch learners of English. In this study she addresses two basic research questions: (a) Are there any differences between L1 and L2 self-repair? and (b) Does L2 self-repair behavior reflect stages of L2 development? The results of this study are clearly laid out in her chapter.

In considering the pedagogical implications of self-repair data, Van Hest argues for the existence of two aspects of self-repair behavior that should be of special interest to language teachers: (a) distribution of self-repair data, and (b) the use of editing terms. Her results suggest that self-repair behavior reflects speakers' ability to assess the correctness and the appropriateness of the language they produce. What gets repaired at different stages appears to be linked to those aspects language learners have already mastered or are on the verge of mastering. This means that self-repair behavior can provide language teachers with useful information about their learners' level of language competence and about the stage of language acquisition those learners have attained.

Her results also indicate that a high percentage of L1 editing terms exists in the speech of beginning L2 speakers. This percentage drops with the increase of language skills. A possible explanation for this phenomenon is that beginning learners are so preoccupied with the production process that they can pay little attention to such aspects as the fluency of their speech or the correct use of editing terms.

Van Hest concludes that the self-repair data that learners produce may be of consequence to assessment specialists as well as language teachers insofar as they provide a linguistic basis for proficiency tests to be geared to the learner's current state of development. In this way, self-repair data can be especially useful in formulating descriptors with respect to interaction, oral production, and spoken fluency, all areas where self-repair is inextricably bound.

PORTFOLIO ASSESSMENT

The value of assessment portfolios as the cornerstone of learner-directed assessment has been well documented in the burgeoning literature on portfolio pedagogy. Sommers (1991), Condon and Hamp-Lyons (1991), and Porter and Cleland (1995), advocates of portfolio assessment, have cited the following contributions of assessment portfolios: enables instruction to be linked to assessment, promotes reflection, helps learners to take responsibility for their own learning, enables learners to see gaps in their learning, and enables learners to take risks. Furthermore, the process-oriented nature of portfolio assessment allows teachers to gauge not only the final product, but also the learners' growth and accomplishments over a period of time.

Equally strong is the support for maintaining portfolios as assessment instruments for students who are linguistically and culturally diverse. As suggested earlier in this chapter, traditional norm-referenced assessment tools have never accurately measured the communicative abilities of second-language learners with precision. Assessment portfolios, as explained in chapter 5, by Margo Gottlieb, allow these learners to showcase their accomplishments, demonstrate originality and creativity, and think critically.

Despite the considerable endorsement of portfolio pedagogy in recent years, there are some areas of concern in the validity and reliability of portfolios as alternatives to traditional assessment tools. One of the major areas of concern is developing consistent guidelines for evaluating the collections in a portfolio. Another thorny issue is selection of the appropriate documents for a portfolio. The aim of the two chapters authored by Gottlieb (chap. 5) and Hirvela and Pierson (chap. 6) is to address the necessary prerequisites leading to the development of reliable assessment portfolios, namely selecting the dimensions of a portfolio, defining its purpose, and establishing the criteria for judging its content.

In her chapter on portfolios in elementary and secondary schools, Gottlieb examines the theoretical background and practical applications of portfolios, which she later applies to second-language learning. In broadening the case for portfolios, Gottlieb indicates that since the 1980s instructional and assessment practices have tended to merge and blend. With assessment becoming more performance-based and classroom-centered, the portfolio has emerged as a personal, multiple-use assessment tool for both teachers and students.

Gottlieb also explains that the expanding notions and functions of portfolios in education call for a more precise definition of the concept. Assessment portfolios should have a clear-cut purpose compatible with defined objectives and standards. Also, an assessment portfolio should be an organized compilation of original student work and their supporting materials chosen in part by the students.

For Gottlieb, learner-directed assessment portfolios are the key to a student-centered curriculum, even though at the institutional level this personalization is diminished. Nevertheless, there is little evidence at the state level in the United States that large-scale assessment has been designed for linguistically and culturally diverse students and there are few substantial policies that determine their participation.

Gottlieb cites a study in which, since the 1991 school year, the concept of portfolios for linguistically and culturally diverse students and their teachers has been incorporated into a graduate-level assessment course that is one of the requirements for ESL/bilingual approval in Illinois. The results of this study indicate that educators have exhibited optimism regarding the potential impact of portfolios on students, including those from linguistically and culturally diverse backgrounds. In her opinion, the initial inflated perceptions of educators as to the blanket usefulness of portfolios appear to have been realistically tamed. Further research on portfolio assessment is needed to provide clarification to stakeholders as to their respective roles and contributions to the assessment process.

Gottlieb believes that equity for students in elementary and secondary schools can be achieved, in part, through reliable, valid, and fair assessment practices. Learner-directed assessment in tandem with portfolio assessment creates a natural flow of information. When assessment assumes an advocacy role, such as in the case of ESL/bilingual education, then the benefits accrued through portfolio use are enabling and facilitating for second-language learners. Assessment portfolios hold a promise for all learners: students, teachers, and administrators.

In their chapter, Hirvela and Pierson treat portfolio assessment in the context of ESL writing instruction and examine the contributions that portfolio pedagogy can make toward ESL learners' authentic self-assessment of their efforts and achievements in the writing classroom. This is accomplished by examining important perspectives on portfolios and assessment. The authors conclude by discussing two university ESL teaching environments in which portfolios have been used as both teacher-assessment and learner self-assessment tools. Although these authors admit no easy consensus exists as to what should comprise a proper portfolio, they do cite in detail the portfolio guidelines that have emerged among specialists in recent decades. Hirvela and Pierson acknowledge that portfolios represent a fundamentally different approach to language assessment, one that enlarges and reshapes the whole notion of what language assessment can and should do. It is an approach that emphasizes performance assessment rather than the traditional summative assessment found in many testing situations. This kind of assessment underscores what students can do rather than just what they know. Hirvela and Pierson argue that student authority or ownership is achieved by allowing them to review and assess their writing in order to decide what pieces they will present to their teachers in their portfolios. Student reflection on their writing in the preparation of the portfolio is a key element in portfolio pedagogy and an essential aspect of learner self-assessment. In addition, revision, also a key element in writing instruction, receives similar attention in portfolio building.

Hirvela and Pierson cite the many uses of portfolios (e.g., placement, gatekeeping, or as a means of assisting in evaluating or grading performance in a specific course). The number of roles has enabled numerous approaches to portfolios to emerge. With these approaches come many questions and choices. A key area is deciding who should determine portfo-lio contents—the teacher, the administrator, or the students themselves. This is a thorny area discussed by Hirvela and Pierson.

Alluding to portfolio techniques they employ with students in their own institutions, Hirvela and Pierson discuss student perceptions of writing as a form of learning when drafting and composing explanations (usually in the form of a letter to their instructor that introduces the contents of the portfolio) of what they have included in their portfolio, and why they have included it. As they write this introductory letter, students, in a real way, are evaluating the worth of their writing. For Hirvela and Pierson, the im-portance of self-evaluation comes from this student reflection, a form of self-assessment intellectually empowering student writers to see what is usually hidden from them in the writing process. This occurs when they ex-amine the materials they have produced in a writing course and decide what to include in their portfolios and how to present it to their readers or teachers.

VERBAL REPORTS

Verbal reports or think-aloud protocols were first employed in first-lan-guage studies as a research technique to investigate the strategies that readers employ to complete a given task (Ericsson & Simon, 1993; Garner, 1982). The successful use of this method of analysis in exploring learners' reading strategies was the impetus for its recognition as a necessary tool in the study of language acquisition and assessment. Recent studies in sec-ond-language reading and assessment have placed more emphasis on the process of reading in a second language than the content of the test and the product.

Among the numerous studies cited in the growing literature of think-aloud protocols is the research conducted by Anderson, Bachman, Perkins, and Cohen (1991). To investigate the construct validity of different item types in reading comprehension tests, this study examines the relationship between learners' strategies and item performance in multiple choice for-mats. The data gained from this study reveals that in selecting answers to difficult questions, many participants used strategies, such as elimination or matching the stems to the text, that did not reflect the understanding of the text, and there was no relation between these strategies and the purpose of the test questions. These findings confirmed in part the concerns raised by the authors (Anderson et al., 1991) that the multiple-choice form of test-ing, the most common method used in standardized testing, is not the most valid format for measuring reading comprehension. This concern is shared by the editors of this volume. We, therefore, expect that the studies reported in this volume and similar publications will assist practitioners in search of more valid assessment tools to move away from the traditional pa-per-and-pencil tests and consider alternative forms of assessment that bear learner representation.

In chapter 7 by Andrew Cohen, the use of verbal reports is extended to an-alyze the speech acts of second-language learners. In his chapter, Cohen in-troduces a refreshing review of the literature on the use of verbal reports to investigate the test-taking strategies that respondents employ in a variety of authentic assessment tasks, such as taking open-ended reading compre-hension tests, writing summaries, and performing complex oral production tasks. Cohen contrasts three forms of verbal reports: (a) self-report (a de-scription by the learner of what he or she does by means of generalized state-ments); (b) self-observation (the inspection of specific language behavior by the learner); and (c) self-revelation (how learner think-aloud protocols disclose their language-processing thoughts while attending to linguistic information). To unravel some of the inconsistencies that are often observed in test results, Cohen reports on various counterproductive strategies that learners employ in test-taking. He cites Gordon's (1987) study that indi-cates that often answering reading comprehension test questions does not necessarily reflect comprehension of the text. In performing oral produc-tion tests, the study of Cohen and Holstein (1993) revealed that in more complex speech acts such as making requests or forming complaints, the re-spondents, often through two languages, searched for language forms and avoided words with which they were uncomfortable.

The second part of Cohen's chapter contains a lengthy focus on ways to enhance verbal reports. Factors such as the length of guidance selection of excerpts, and the language of choice are examined in depth and their role in enhancing the outcomes of verbal reports are discussed. The insights gained from Cohen's chapter are especially beneficial to those responsible for con-structing and administering assessment instruments.

In revisiting verbal reports, Cohen reveals the respondents' test-taking strategies that could lead assessment specialists to improved revision of test items and more accurate interpretation of test results. He also provides guidelines for a more rigorous design for investigating and interpreting such strategies. Moreover, the respondents, for the most part, viewed the process of verbal reports as a positive learning experience. The process of verbalizing their thoughts enhanced their awareness and assessment of vari-ous aspects of reading. Cohen cites a study conducted by Crutcher (1990) in which positive effects of verbal reports in the area of vocabulary learning and retention were reported. The positive feedback from the learner con-firms yet another advantage of engaging respondents in the process of test development—the pedagogical value of learner-directed assessment.

Cohen provides the classroom teachers with guidelines for utilizing ver-bal report methods in pair and group works aimed at identifying the strategies respondents use to produce answers to test questions. The information gained from such exercises can assist classroom teachers in examining their exams or testing the tests.

In summary, this volume has been written to assist ESL practitioners, especially classroom teachers and program directors, in search of enhanced methods of evaluation. We hope the insight gained from the chapters in this volume will encourage a shift toward learner-directed assessment.

Chapter 2

Defining a Flexible Common Measurement Scale: Descriptors for Self and Teacher Assessment

Brian North
Eurocentres Foundation, Zürich

Presently, developments in Europe are moving toward the adoption of a European framework of common levels. Such an idea is not entirely novel in the United States, where the search for a common metric is, as Bachman commented (1990), a common thread running through much recent literature on language testing. In the United States, the need to maintain the momentum toward such a common framework "with all of its difficulties" has been described as "essential for the development of a meaningful national language policy in foreign language learning and use" (Lambert, 1993, p. 155) and such a framework has been also proposed as a means of comparing research outcomes (Clark & O'Mara, 1991, p. 83). In Europe, the motivation for a common framework (or metric) is more pragmatic, more sociopolitical than academic. In a world of greatly increased international communications and trade, personal mobility and the interrupted schooling and lifelong learning that it entails, such a framework (Trim, 1978, 1992) could facilitate comparison between systems; describe achievement in terms meaningful to teachers, learners, parents, and employers (Schneider & Richtereich, 1992); and allow learners to plot a personal record of achievement during their language-learning career across different institutions (Schärer, 1992).

The aim of the Council of Europe Proposal for a Common European Framework of Reference for Language Learning and Teaching (Council of

Europe, 1996) was actually considerably wider than the common metric yardstick American Council on the Teaching of Foreign Languages/Interagency Round Table (ACTFL/ILR) project. The draft framework proposal is an initial step toward providing curriculum planners with a comprehensive categorization of the parameters involved in communicative competence with illustrative scales of proficiency for those parameters that appear to be scaleable. The draft scales of proficiency defining different aspects of language competence at different levels that are included in the framework are based on research in Switzerland. Indeed, Switzerland hosted, and Eurocentres coordinated, the Council of Europe intergovernmental symposium "Transparency and Coherence in Language Learning in Europe: Objectives, Evaluation and Certification" (Council of Europe, 1992) that recommended the development of a common framework. The Swiss proposal at that conference was the development of a kind of language passport that would enable learners to keep track of where they were in learning the language and that would make sense to all employers, because it reported achievement on a common scale. The expression *language portfolio* was adopted to replace passport because it was increasingly felt that such an instrument, although primarily a reporting document, could also serve as an orientation during the learning process. The symposium unanimously recommended the development of the framework, and "of subsequently a European Language Portfolio allowing individuals to report their language learning achievement in terms of a Common European Scale related to the Framework" (Council of Europe, 1992, p. 40). This recommendation has since been accepted by the Council of Ministers. It also appears as if the European Commission (EU) may adopt the framework and common scale it proposes in order to avoid duplication of effort.

The aims of the Swiss research project were to:

1. Develop clear, relevant, and useable descriptors for different categories related to those put forward in the common framework through extensive consultation with teachers and then to calibrate the best descriptors empirically for the first draft of a common European scale.
2. Develop prototype self and teacher assessment instruments to launch experimentation in Switzerland with the language portfolio recording achievement in relation to the common European scale.

The project was based on two models: (a) the descriptive scheme put forward in the Council of Europe framework that draws on models of competence and proficiency (e.g., Bachman, 1990; Canale & Swain, 1980; North, 1994a; Van Ek, 1986); and (b) the Rasch Item Response Theory measurement model (Woods & Baker, 1985; Wright & Stone, 1979) in its scalar form (Wright & Masters, 1982), using a variant that takes account of assessor subjectivity (Linacre, 1989) to assess learner proficiency. The methodology adopted is a development of that proposed by North (1993a), inspired by Kenyon's use of the Linacre model in relation to ACTFL (Kenyon & Stanfield, 1992).

The research had two phases, a pilot and a main phase. The pilot phase, which was mounted in 1994, dealt with interactive spoken English, whereas the main phase, which was mounted in 1995, dealt with interactive spoken French, noninteractive German listening, and reading in English.

The survey of English conducted in 1994 to pilot the methodology was the subject of a doctoral thesis (North, 1995); the full text is expected be published shortly (Schneider, North, & Richtereich, in press). The project followed a broadly similar pattern of three phases each year: (a) the creation of a descriptor pool of aproximately 1,000 items each year using a relatively comprehensive review of some 35 existing scales of language proficiency undertaken for the Council of Europe (North, 1993b) as a starting point; (b) qualitative validation of descriptors in a series of approximately 30 workshops with teachers through repertory grid analysis of the metalanguage teachers used to discuss video performances and through sorting tasks organizing draft descriptors into categories; and (c) quantitative validation of a selection of the descriptors interpreted most consistently in the workshops through Rasch analysis of teachers' assessment of their learners' proficiency on a checklist or questionnaire, plus their ratings of performances on video recordings at all levels. One hundred English teachers from different educational sectors rated 945 learners in 1994, and in the second year, 192 teachers (81 French teachers, 65 German teachers, 46 English teachers) participated.

In the implementation phase launched at a conference in September 1996, teachers in the network created by the project were invited to experiment with the descriptors in continuous assessment instruments for teacher and learner use (e.g., checklists; Oskarson, 1978, and profile grids; see Brindley, 1989, for a review of formats) as part of the move toward the development of a European language portfolio.

SCALING PROFICIENCY DESCRIPTORS

The creation of a transparent, coherent framework of defined levels and categories presupposes assigning descriptions of language proficiency to one level or another—that is *scaling* descriptors. Considering the extent of the literature on scaling and on behavioral scaling in particular (e.g., Borman, 1986; Landy & Farr, 1983; Smith & Kendall, 1963), it is in fact surprising how little use has been made of scaling theory or of empirical development in the production of language proficiency scales, virtually all of which appear to have been produced on the basis of intuition by a single author or small committee (see North, 1993b, for reviews). Yet subjectivity in assessment with reference to defined criteria occurs in two quite separate ways.

First, and most obvious, raters vary widely in their severity and this lack of consistency can account for as much as 40% of test variance (Cason & Cason, 1984; Linacre, 1989), which is why assessment approaches involving two assessors are increasingly common. Second, however, the assignment of a descriptor to a level by the author(s) systematizes subjective error on the part of the author(s) so that even if raters are trained to assess the same way (to reduce the difference in severity between them) the validity of the assessment is still questionable—and reliability will be hard to achieve as those descriptors that are poorly defined or incorrectly placed on the scale will undermine the assessors efforts. Although intuitively developed scales of proficiency may work in an in-house assessment approach for a specific context with a familiar population of learners and assessors, reliance on author intuition has been criticized in relation to the development of national framework scales of language proficiency (e.g., Bachman & Savignon, 1986; Brindley, 1986, 1991, in relation to the Australian Second Language Proficiency Ratings [ASLPR]; Fulcher, 1987, 1993, in relation to the British ELTS; Lantolf & Frawley, 1985, 1988; Skehan, 1984; Spolsky, 1986, 1993, in relation to the American Council on the Teaching of Foreign Languages [ACTFL] Guidelines). The problem is well known in the scaling literature and led Thurstone (cited in Wright & Masters, 1983) to propose that:

> The scale values of the statements should not be affected by the opinions of the people who helped to construct it (the scale). This may turn out to be a severe test in practice, but the scaling method must stand such a test before it can be accepted as being more than a description of the people who construct the scale. At any rate, to the extent that the present method of scale construction is affected by the opinions of the readers who help sort out the original statements into a scale, to that extent the validity of the scale may be challenged. (p. 15)

For the development of a scale that is intended to serve as a point of reference for different educational sectors, linguistic areas, and target languages, these problems are particularly acute. No small group of readers would be sufficiently representative to arrive at generalizable scale values, no informants could provide information about the way in which descriptors perform when actually used to assess the learners in question. A Rasch analysis calibrates the items (here descriptors of proficiency) and the persons (here language learners) onto an arithmetical scale and, to the extent that new groups of learners can be considered to be further groups of the original assessment population rather than new populations, Rasch theory claims scale values to be constant, "instrument-free," "person-free" objective (Wright & Linacre, 1987, p. 2). In addition, by working at an item level, the approach offers the opportunity to identify those items (here descriptors) or people who do not fit with the main construct being measured and exclude them if desired in order to increase the accuracy of the calibration of the difficulty values for those descriptors that are consistent and reliable and the calibration of the learner proficiency values from those teacher ratings that are consistent and credible. Those proficiency values can also be adjusted to take account of the degree of severity or lenience of the assessor (Linacre, 1989), offering the possibility of something close to objective measurement of subjective judgments.

RESULTS

The data analysis has produced: (a) a defined 10-band scale of language proficiency, regrouped into six levels for the Council of Europe framework; (b) a bank of classified, calibrated descriptors covering a relatively large number of categories related to the Council of Europe framework; and (c) an impression of what factors make descriptors work.

A Defined Scale

The descriptors are calibrated in rank order on a logic scale. Levels are created by establishing cut-off points on the scale. Setting cut-offs is always a subjective decision. As Jaeger (1989) stated: "No amount of data collection, data analysis and model building can replace the ultimate judgmental act of deciding which performances are meritorious or acceptable and which are unacceptable or inadequate" (p. 492), or as Wright and Grosse (1993, p. 316) said: "No measuring system can decide for us at what point *short* becomes *tall*." The decision to report 10 levels is, however, far from arbitrary. First, as Pollitt (1991) showed, there is a relation between the reliability of a data set and the number of levels it will bear; second, these cut-offs are set at almost exactly equal intervals on the measurement scale; and finally a comparative analysis of the calibration of the content elements that appear in descriptors (e.g., topics that can handled; degree of help required) and detailed consideration of the formulation of adjacent descriptors shows a remarkable degree of coherence inside these levels—and an apparently qualitative change at these cut-off points.

The scale of 10 levels was produced in the 1994 analysis for English, focusing on interaction and spoken production. One of the functions of the 1995 survey was to replicate the 1994 finding, and determine whether the scale remained stable when French and German teachers were also included in the analysis rating in relation to French-German translations. To enable equating, 70 items from the 1994 English survey were reused in 1995 as mentioned previously, and the 1995 data were analyzed both with the 70 descriptors from 1994 anchored to the difficulty values established in 1994, and separately. The difficulty values for the items in the main listening and speaking scale proved to be very stable. Only 8 of the 70 descriptors calibrated in 1994 and reused in 1995 to anchor the 1995 data to that from 1994 were in fact interpreted in a significantly different way in 1995 (i.e., fell outside the criterion line). After the removal of those eight descriptors, the values of the 108 listening and speaking items used in 1995 (now including only 62 from 1994), when analyzed separately and when analyzed with the 62 common items, anchored to their 1994 values correlated 0.992 (Pearson). This is a very satisfactory consistency between the two years when considering that: (a) 1994 values were based on 100 English teachers, whereas in 1995 only 46 of the 192 teachers taught English, thus the ratings dominating the 1995 construct were those of the French and German teachers; (b) the questionnaire forms used for data collection were completely different in the 2 years with four forms in 1995 covering the ground covered by seven in 1994; (c) the majority of teachers were using the descriptors in French or German in the second year, so the problems with those eight descriptors may have been at least partly caused by inadequate translation.

A Classified Descriptor Bank

Not all of the categories originally included could be successfully calibrated. Sometimes this was due to a lack of unidimensionality. As Henning (1992) discussed, tests can exhibit sufficient psychometric unidimensionality without any justifiable assumptions about psychological unidimensionality. In other words, dimensionality in Rasch, for example, has a technical meaning related to the technical meaning of reliability as separability. Are the items strung out nicely along the 45 degrees of a plot, or are some items pulling away to the sides because they do not really fit the main construct created by the data? Removal of such outliers clarifies the picture and increases the scale length, the reliability, and the precision of the difficulty values for the items—in this case descriptors. Unlike classical test theory (CTT: reliability theory) item response theory (IRT: Rasch) does not say such outliers are necessarily bad items—but rather that they do not belong here and should perhaps be analyzed separately to see if they build their own construct.

Four groups of categories were actually lost:

1. Sociocultural competence: It is not clear how much this problem was caused by the concept being separate from language proficiency (and hence not fitting), by rather vague descriptors identified as problematic in the workshops, or by inconsistent responses by the teachers.

2. Those descriptors relating to (in)dependence on or from interlocutor accommodation (need for simplification; need to get repetition or clarification) that are implicitly negative concepts. These aspects worked better as provisos at the end of positive statements focusing on what the

learner could do (e.g., can understand what is said clearly, slowly, and directly to him or her in simple everyday conversation; can be made to understand, if the speaker can take the trouble).

3. Those asking teachers to guess about activities (generally work-related) beyond their direct experience; telephoning; attending formal meetings, giving formal presentations; writing reports and essays; formal correspondence. This could be a problem of dimensionality (as with reading and sociocultural competence) or it could be that teachers were just unable to give the information. Griffin (1989, 1990) reported a similar problem in relation to library activities during the development of his primary school reading scale.

4. Reading Literature: Four descriptors included in year 2—the lowest concerning following the storyline of an extended narrative—all proved to be unstable: to be interpreted differently on adjacent questionnaires. This could be related to the categories listed in the previous group or one could see the problem as related to culture—and hence, sociocultural competence.

However, the categories for which descriptors were successfully validated and calibrated still offer a relatively rich metalanguage:

A. Communicative Activities

1. Global language use
   a) Overall interaction
2. Listening
   a) Overall listening comprehension
   b) Receptive listening
      i. Listening to announcements and instructions
      ii. Listening as a member of an audience
      iii. Listening to radio and audio recordings
      iv. Watching TV and film
   c) Interactive listening
      i. Comprehension in spoken interaction
3. Reading
   a) Overall reading comprehension
      i. Reading instructions
      ii. Reading for information
      iii. Reading for orientation (skimming, scanning)
   b) Interaction: transactional
      i. Service encounters and negotiations
      ii. Information exchange

      iii. Interviewing and being interviewed
      iv. Notes, messages and forms
    c) Interpersonal interaction
      i. Conversation
      ii. Discussion
      iii. Personal correspondence
    d) Production (spoken)
      i. Description
    e) Sustained monologue
      i. Putting a case

B. Strategies

1. Reception strategies
    a) Identifying cues and inferring
    b) Interaction strategies
      i. Turntaking
      ii. Cooperating
      iii. Asking for clarification
    c) Production strategies
      i. Planning
      ii. Compensating
      iii. Repairing and monitoring

C. Aspects of Communicative Language Proficiency

1. Pragmatic
    a) Fluency
    b) Language use
      i. Flexibility
      ii. Coherence
      iii. Thematic development
      iv. Precision
2. Linguistic
    a) General range
    b) Language
      i. Vocabulary range
      ii. Grammatical accuracy
      iii. Vocabulary control
      iv. Pronunciation

CONCLUSIONS ON DESCRIPTORS

The overall impression gained on what makes a descriptor work is summarized in the following list of points:

1. Positiveness: This is a common characteristic on assessor-orientated scales (Alderson, 1991)—dealing with aspects of communicative language proficiency rather than tasks the learner can or should be able to perform (user- or constructor-oriented)—for the formulation of entries at lower levels to be negatively worded. It is more difficult to formulate proficiency at low levels in terms of what the learner can do rather than in terms of what he or she cannot do, but if a set of scaled levels of proficiency are to serve as objectives rather than as an instrument for screening candidates into grade groups, then positive formulation is desirable.

2. Definiteness: Descriptors should describe concrete features of performance, concrete tasks, and/or concrete degrees of skill in performing tasks. There are two points here. First, the descriptor should avoid vagueness, for example, "can use a range of appropriate strategies." This would lead to questions about the meaning of a strategy, what strategies are appropriate, and the interpretation of "range." The problem with vague descriptors is that they can read quite nicely, but an apparent ease of acceptance can mask the fact that everyone is interpreting them differently. Second, distinctions between steps on a scale should not be dependent on replacing a qualifier like "some" or "a few" with "many" or "most" or by replacing "fairly broad" with "very broad" or "moderate" with "good" at the next level up (Champney, 1941). Distinctions should be real, not word-processed, and this may mean gaps where meaningful, concrete distinctions cannot be made.

3. Clarity: Descriptors should be transparent—not dense, verbose, or jargon-ridden. Apart from the barrier to understanding, it is sometimes the case that when jargon is stripped away, an apparently impressive descriptor can turn out to be saying very little. Second, they should be written in simple syntax with an explicit logical structure. Double-barreled descriptors ("can do X but cannot do Y") appear to be less easy for teachers to relate to. This may be because they combine a positive with a negative—and only one may be true of the person concerned; it may be because of the breach of the positiveness requirement. Fundamentally, however, any two clause sentences linked by "and" or "but" should be examined carefully to determine if they should be split; three-clause sentences appear to be too complex.

4. Brevity: There is a school of thought that achieves definiteness by a very comprehensive listing that is intended to transmit a detailed portrait of what raters can recognize as a typical learner at the level concerned (ASLPR, ILR). Teachers in this project, however, consistently preferred short descriptors and tended to reject or split descriptors longer than

about 20 words—approximately two lines of normal type. Oppenheim (1992) also recommended up to approximately 20 words.

5. Independence: Descriptors should describe a criterion behavior—that one can say *Yes* or *No* to the question of whether the person can do this (Skehan, 1984). Descriptors should not be dependent for meaning on the formulation of other descriptors on the scale.

EXPLOITATION

The bank of descriptors produced during the Swiss research project and included in the Council of Europe framework document is a resource, not an instrument. Like an item bank, the bank is classified by content categories, and calibrated for difficulty in relation to a particular (in this case multilingual and multisector) context. Like an item bank, the descriptor bank can be used to derive assessment instruments.

Caveats

However, in producing those instruments, individual descriptors in the bank may need to be combined, adapted, extended, and added to for the instruments derived from the bank to function satisfactorily for a particular function in a particular context. Also, although items from an item bank are objective in that no subjective judgment should be required to mark them (although somebody wrote them of course), descriptors have to be interpreted to be used. Despite the scaling of the descriptors according to consensus interpretation in a multisector environment, this poses three problems:

1. An assessment instrument exploiting the descriptors may be presenting them in a context different to the one in which they were calibrated (a problem affecting all item banking and examination pretesting).
2. People are people, and no two people understand exactly the same thing by the same formulation—everybody has a different degree of leniency or severity—although differences can be at least moderated by training.
3. Teachers naturally focus on their class and therefore often exaggerate differences between individuals that are irrelevant in terms of the steps on a common scale.

That is to say, a priori validation of the descriptors included in a scale is a developmental step that does not replace the need for a postieri validation of final assessment instruments presenting the scale in the context in which it is to be used; a test is not valid—it is valid for something (Henning, 1990). Experiences in Eurocentres with the application of a common framework in centers teaching European languages only in areas where the languages are spoken (i.e., different pedagogic cultures) suggests that the consistency of judgments in relation to common written statements is greatly increased by the following:

1. Existence of content information in the form of language specifications derived from scale levels, information used to rate books and other materials onto the scale which helps to give the levels a pedagogic reality.

2. Written statements that are supplemented with benchmark samples on video that are used for training (as with ACTFL packs) in order to reduce variation of severity.

3. Utilization of results from tests drawn from an item bank (Eurocentres, 1997; Jones, 1993) equated to the same scale to dampen the often reported phenomenon of teachers claiming too much space on a common scale for their particular class: a form of excessive reliability (in the sense of separability) caused by norm-referencing ("She's better than him so I'd better put her a bit higher"). Standardized scaled Key Stage tests in the English National Curriculum are also playing this role in helping teachers adopt a common interpretation of levels on the National Curriculum scale when they grade course work, similar to U.S. portfolio assessment (Pollitt, personal communication, 1994).

Formats

There are three principal ways of physically organizing descriptors on paper, although each has endless variations: (a) a holistic scale: bands on top of another, (b) a profiling grid: categories defined at a series of bands, and (c) a checklist: individual descriptors presented as a separate criterion statement. These three formats exploiting descriptors calibrated in the project are illustrated in the appendix with two examples of each, as follows:

Scales

1. A global scale—all skills, six main levels adopted for Council of Europe framework; (Note: the names of levels are going to be replaced by a numbering system because they are untranslatable!).

2. A holistic scale for spoken interaction, showing the full 10-level empirical scale developed in the Swiss research project; the bottom level "Tourist" is an ability to perform specific isolated tasks, and is not presented as a level in the Council of Europe framework; the "Plus" levels are referred to in the framework as an option for particular contexts, but the political consensus is to adopt the six levels.

Grid

1. A grid profiling proficiency in communicative activities, centered on threshold level shows only a limited range of levels, defines plus levels.
2. A grid profiling qualitative aspects of proficiency used to rate video performances at a conference launching the portfolio (see later) shows the full range of levels, but does not define "plus levels" due partly to fears of causing cognitive overload in what was an initiation session.

Checklist

1. A teacher assessment checklist used as a data-collection instrument during Year 1 contains items that turned out to be at different levels. Those of the original 50 items that were rejected during analysis are given in italics.
2. A self-assessment checklist taken from the first draft of the portfolio (see following) contains only items calibrated at this level, reformulated, if necessary, for self-assessment.

A LANGUAGE PORTFOLIO FOR REPORTING ACHIEVEMENT

The results of the research project have been exploited as discussed previously to prepare a prototype for a portfolio, which was the subject of a conference in Fribourg in 1996. The portfolio has been produced in the three main Swiss national languages of German, French, and Italian, because it is intended to be used in the mother tongue, as well as English. The fourth Swiss national language, Romansch, is spoken only in parts of the Alpine region in a series of very small distinct speech communities. Proficiency in all languages are intended to be recorded in the portfolio, but there are practical limitations to the number of versions which can be reliably produced, at least initially.

In its initial form the portfolio has the following main sections, although this may change:

1. An overview that offers a self-assessment grid defining listening, reading spoken interaction, spoken production (monologue) and writing at the six Council of Europe main levels. Learners use this to determine their skill level and describe what examinations, certificates, and attestations support this. The overview also helps learners (or their teachers) decide which checklists (see later) are appropriate. Increasingly, this is becoming a common core.

2. The passport section. This section includes: (a) copies of certificates with a description of relevant exams; (b) an official form relating the exam(s) in question to the common levels; and (c) attestation of other language-learning experiences like exchange trips, language courses, playing host to a foreign visitor, and participating in interactive international projects, and so forth.

3. Self-assessment checklists of descriptors at different levels. Learners use these checklists to: (a) explain what they think they can do, and (b) what they feel is their priority objective. These checklists are the most direct application of the descriptors scaled in the research project.

4. A dossier. In the dossier learners can, if they wish, outline their learner biographies and provide examples of work, projects, and so on, similar to American learning portfolios.

In addition, the portfolio is supported by a video of speaking performances calibrated during the project.

TEACHER EXPLOITATION OF DESCRIPTOR FORMATS

There is a natural hierarchy among the three formats discussed earlier and illustrated in the appendixes. A grid prioritizes and summarizes the relevant information, which might be available in its complete form in checklists. A scale prioritizes and summarizes the content in a notional grid of categories, even if the writer is not consciously aware of the constituent categories.

Teachers can use the different formats in the following ways. Scales like those given in Appendixes A and B are very useful for establishing reference points. When they are formulated in accessible language focusing on real-life capabilities, they can be useful for self-assessment, negotiating a target level to be the subject of a learning contract, or for reporting results to people outside the system like employers, parents, or admission tutors in a higher education institution. They also enable a group of nonspecialists to discuss relatively quickly what the typical level of attainment, the criterion level of a particular qualification in a particular context may mean in terms of real-life proficiency skills. This is indeed the way in which a holistic scale is used in the portfolio.

Care should be taken not to use a scale such as the two shown in order to directly assess a performance. This is because the descriptors selected are user-oriented (Alderson, 1991), talking about general real-life capabilities. There is little said about the quality that is expected in a spoken or written performance.

Grids are very useful both for more discriminating self-assessment and for teacher assessment of the work's quality. The self-assessment grid shown in Appendix C again focuses on communicative activities and is user-oriented. It does not cover all possible proficiency levels because it is intended to be used in a particular sector. The aim of such an instrument is to encourage learners to assess where they think they are at the moment for each of the language skills, where they think they would like to be at the end of the course, and what relative priority the different language skills have for them. The process of taking part in such a discussion can have a galvanizing effect on learner motivation. It can also encourage the teacher leading such a discussion to reevaluate the program and materials available in terms of their utility in relation to such practical language goals.

The second grid (see Appendix D) is quite different. It is assessor-oriented (Alderson, 1991) and focuses on the quality of the language being displayed in the assessed performance. The criteria for judgment are transparent. In this case, range (complexity of language, breadth of vocabulary for different topics), accuracy (grammatical control and self correction), fluency, interaction (ability to turntake and to weave their contribution into joint discourse), and coherence (ability to connect speech into cohesive discourse). This grid was produced for a particular event. Pronunciation is deliberately missing. Range, accuracy, and fluency could be regarded as the three fundamental qualitative aspects of second-language use. Interaction and coherence were added because this particular spoken assessment task had a student–student interaction task (interaction) and a semiprepared monologue task (coherence).

The grid offers, but does not define plus levels between the main levels. The levels given provide sufficient reference points—one does not necessarily need to define every level verbally for people to be able to use the grid. Forcing distinctions where they are difficult to define may in fact be counterproductive.

Different aims or different test tasks may require different criteria. The grid may be used primarily in training, as a reference document for assessors negotiating a grade or in live assessment. When a grid is used for live assessment, consensus experience is that four to five categories is the practical maximum. Alternatively, the descriptors could be merged into a scale of short holistic statements for use during the actual assessment in order to lighten the cognitive load. However, the process of using a grid to negotiate common grades for a piece of work confronts teachers with the fact that everyone has a lead factor that tends to over influence their holistic judgment.

Checklists are useful for listing key communicative tasks, but there is no reason why key qualities or key strategies should not be included. Checklists can be used for assessment and self-assessment, as with the examples given as Appendixes E and F. They can be used in a forward-looking role (constructor-oriented; Alderson, 1991) as reminders of key content that can be referred to for planning a course or designing an assessment task. Alternatively, they can be used for reflection in what is often referred to as a log book (this is what we covered).

When selecting a format and formulation for descriptors, it is fundamental to: (a) keep in mind and indicate clearly the purpose for which the instrument created is to be used; (b) simplify the first version written; (c) collect locally relevant samples of performance to illustrate the levels described; and (d) compare typical examples from such samples with the relevant formulations in order to polish these and to highlight in a second edition the features that are particularly salient in the context concerned.

NOTE

This chapter relates to a paper given at the Language Testing Research Colloquium in Tampere, Finland, in 1996. However, space here has been used to contextualize the project referred to for a U.S. audience, to discuss exploitation of the results, and to provide practitioners with illustrations of formats for possible assessment instruments. This is all at the expense of the discussion of the scaling issues involved, which was the focus of the LTRC paper. For technical scaling issues, readers are therefore referred to the original LTRC paper and to other works cited here.

APPENDIX A
GLOBAL SCALE

Adopted for the draft proposal for a Council of Europe common framework

---

Mastery

Can understand with ease virtually everything heard or read. Can summarize information from different spoken and written sources, reconstructing arguments and accounts in a coherent presentation. Can express him- or herself spontaneously and very fluently and precisely, differentiating finer shades of meaning even in more complex situations.

Effective Operational Proficiency

Can understand a wide range of demanding, longer texts, and recognize implicit meaning. Can express him or herself fluently and spontaneously without much obvious searching for expressions. Can use language flexibly and effectively for social, academic, and professional purposes. Can produce clear, well-structured, and detailed text on complex subjects, showing controlled use of organizational patterns, connectors, and cohesive devices.

Vantage

Can understand the main ideas of complex text on both concrete and abstract topics, including technical discussions in his or her field of specialization. Can interact with a degree of fluency and spontaneity that makes regular interaction with native speakers quite possible without strain for either party. Can produce clear, detailed text on a wide range of subjects and explain a viewpoint on a topical issue giving the advantages and disadvantages of various options.

Threshold

Can understand the main points of clear standard input on familiar matters regularly encountered in work, school, leisure, and so on. Can deal with most situations likely to arise while traveling in an area where the language is spoken. Can produce simple, connected text on topics that are familiar or of personal interest. Can describe experiences and events, dreams, hopes, and ambitions and briefly give reasons and explanations for opinions and plans.

Waystage

Can understand sentences and frequently used expressions related to areas of most immediate relevance (e.g., very basic personal and family information, shopping, local geography, employment). Can communicate in simple and routine tasks requiring a simple and direct exchange of information on familiar and routine matters. Can describe in simple terms, aspects of his or her background, immediate environment, and matters in areas of immediate need.

Breakthrough

Can understand and use familiar everyday expressions and very basic phrases aimed at the satisfaction of needs of a concrete type. Can introduce him- or herself and others and can ask and answer questions about personal details such as where he or she lives, people he or she knows, and things he or she has. Can interact in a simple way provided the other person talks slowly and clearly and is prepared to help.

APPENDIX B
HOLISTIC SCALE FOR INTERACTION

INTERACTION
[A holistic scale summarizing descriptor content]

Mastery

Has a good command of idiomatic expressions and colloquialisms with
awareness of connotative levels of meaning. Can convey finer shades of
meaning precisely by using, with reasonable accuracy, a wide range of
modification devices. Can backtrack and restructure around a difficulty
so smoothly the interlocutor is hardly aware of it.

Effective Operational Proficiency

Can express him or herself fluently and spontaneously, almost effort-
lessly. Has a good command of a broad lexical repertoire allowing gaps to
be readily overcome with circumlocutions. There is little obvious
searching for expressions or avoidance strategies; only a conceptually
difficult subject can hinder a natural, smooth flow of language.

Vantage Plus

Can use the language fluently, accurately, and effectively on a wide range
of general, academic, vocational, or leisure topics, marking clearly the
relations between ideas. Can communicate spontaneously with good
grammatical control without much sign of having to restrict what he or
she wants to say, adopting a level of formality appropriate to the circumstances.

Vantage

Can interact with a degree of fluency and spontaneity that makes regular
interaction with native speakers quite possible without imposing strain
on either party. Can highlight the personal significance of events and experiences and account for and sustain views clearly by providing relevant
explanations and arguments.

Threshold Plus

Can communicate with some confidence on familiar routine and non-
routine matters related to his or her interests and professional field. Can
exchange, check and confirm information, deal with less routine situations, and explain why something is a problem. Can express thoughts on
more abstract, cultural topics such as films, books, music, and so on.

Threshold

Can exploit a wide range of simple language to deal with most situations
likely to arise during travel. Can enter unprepared into conversation on
familiar topics, express personal opinions, and exchange information on

topics that are familiar, of personal interest, or pertinent to everyday life (e.g., family, hobbies, work, travel, and current events).

Waystage Plus

Can interact with reasonable ease in structured situations and short conversations, provided the other person helps if necessary. Can manage simple, routine exchanges without undue effort; can ask and answer questions and exchange ideas and information on familiar topics in predictable everyday situations.

Waystage

Can communicate in simple and routine tasks requiring a simple and direct exchange of information on familiar matters dealing with work and free time. Can handle very short social exchanges but is rarely able to understand enough to keep conversation going of his or her own accord.

Breakthrough

Can interact in a simple way but communication is totally dependent on repetition at a slower rate of speech, rephrasing and repair. Can ask and answer simple questions, initiate and respond to simple statements in areas of immediate need or on very familiar topics.

Tourist

Can ask and tell the date and time of day, follow short, simple directions, and make simple purchases where pointing or other gesture can support the verbal reference.

APPENDIX C
SELF-ASSESSMENT PROFILING GRID: COMMUNICATIVE ACTIVITIES: SPOKEN LANGUAGE
PARTIAL RANGE OF LEVEL: CENTERED ON THRESHOLD

	Waystage	Waystage Plus	Threshold	Threshold Plus	Vantage
Comprehension	I can understand what is said clearly, slowly, and directly to me in simple everyday conversation; I can be made to understand, if the speaker takes the trouble.	I can generally identify the topic of discussion around me that is conducted slowly and clearly. I can generally understand clear, standard speech on familiar matters directed at me, provided I can ask for repetition or reformulation from time to time.	I can generally follow the main points of extended discussion around me, provided speech is clearly articulated in standard dialect. I can follow clearly articulated speech directed at me in everyday conversation, although I sometimes have to ask for repetition of particular words and phrases.	I can, with some effort, catch much of what is said around me, but may find it difficult to participate effectively in discussion with several native speakers who do not modify their language in any way. I can understand what is said directly to me, provided the speaker avoids very idiomatic usage and articulates clearly.	I can follow discussions with several interlocutors on most general themes and on matters related to my field, identifying accurately the key points expressing a point of view. I can understand in detail what is said to me in the standard spoken language even in a noisy environment.
Conversation	I can handle very short social exchanges but am rarely able to understand enough to keep conversation going of my own accord.	I can participate in short conversations in routine contexts on topics of interest.	I can enter unprepared into conversations on familiar topics. I can maintain a conversation or discussion but may sometimes be difficult to follow when trying to say exactly what I would like to.	I can interact competently on informal social occasions. I can maintain conversation with unfamiliar people (e.g., visitors) on subjects of immediate relevance or areas related to my interests or field.	I can engage in extended conversation on most general topics in a clearly participatory fashion, even in a noisy environment. I can sustain interactions with native speakers without requiring them to behave other than the way they would behave with a native speaker.

Transaction	I can communicate in simple and routine tasks requiring a simple and direct exchange of limited information on familiar and routine topics connected with common matters to do with work and free time. I can make simple transactions in shops, post offices, banks, and so on.	I can make myself understood and exchange information on familiar topics connected with common aspects of everyday living such as travel, accommodation, eating, and shopping.	I can understand, exchange, check and confirm, and summarize straightforward factual information and deal with difficult, less routine situations, although I may occasionally have to ask for repetition if the other person's response is rapid or extended.	I can understand and exchange detailed information reliably, explain a problem and make it clear in a disagreement that a concession is necessary.
Discussion	I can discuss everyday practical issues in a simple way when addressed clearly, slowly, and directly.	I can say what I think about things when addressed directly, provided I can ask for repetition of key points if necessary.	I can discuss topics of interest. I can express belief, opinion, agreement, and disagreement politely.	I can explain why something is a problem, and can compare and contrast different alternative suggestions or solutions, commenting on the views of others.	I can take an active part in formal and informal discussion and put a point of view clearly. I can account for and sustain my opinions by providing relevant explanations, arguments, and comments.
Description	I can describe my family, living conditions, education, or most recent job.	I can describe everyday aspects of my surroundings and background (e.g., people, places, a job, or study experience). I can describe plans and arrangements, habits and routines, likes and dislikes, past activities, and personal experiences.	I can give detailed accounts of experiences and real or imaginary events, and can narrate stories and film/book storylines, describing feelings and reactions. I can also describe dreams, hopes, and ambitions.	I can give straightforward descriptions on a variety of familiar subjects within my field of interest. I can describe in detail unpredictable occurrences. (e.g., an accident).	I can give clear, detailed descriptions on a wide range of subjects related to his or her field of interest.

APPENDIX D
TEACHER ASSESSMENT GRID: ASPECTS OF SPOKEN PERFORMANCE:

	RANGE	ACCURACY	FLUENCY	INTERACTION	COHERENCE
M	Shows great flexibility reformulating ideas in differing linguistic forms to convey finer shades of meaning precisely, to give emphasis, to differentiate, and to eliminate ambiguity. Also has a good command of idiomatic expressions and colloquialisms.	Maintains consistent grammatical control of complex language, even while attention is otherwise engaged (e.g., in forward planning, in monitoring others' reactions).	Can express him or herself spontaneously at length with a natural colloquial flow, avoiding or backtracking around any difficulty so smoothly that the interlocutor is hardly aware of it.	Can interact with ease and skill, picking up and using nonverbal and intonational cues apparently effortlessly. Can interweave his or her contribution into the joint discourse with fully natural turntaking, referencing, allusion making, and so on.	Can create coherent and cohesive discourse making full and appropriate use of a variety of organizational patterns and a wide range of connectors and other cohesive devices.
E	Has a good command of a broad range of language allowing him or her to select a formulation to express him or herself clearly in an appropriate style on a wide range of general, academic, professional, or leisure topics without having to restrict what he or she wants to say.	Consistently maintains a high degree of grammatical accuracy; errors are rare, difficult to spot, and generally corrected when they do occur.	Can express him or herself fluently and spontaneously, almost effortlessly. Only a conceptually difficult subject can hinder a natural, smooth flow of language.	Can select a suitable phrase from a readily available range of discourse functions to preface his or her remarks appropriately in order to get or to keep the floor and to relate his or her own contributions skillfully to those of other speakers.	Can produce clear, smoothly flowing, well-structured speech, showing controlled use of organizational patterns, connectors, and cohesive devices.

V+					
V	Has a sufficient range of language to be able to give clear descriptions and express viewpoints on most general topics, without much conspicuous searching for words, using some complex sentence forms to do so.	Shows a relatively high degree of grammatical control. Does not make errors that cause misunderstanding, and can correct most of his or her mistakes.	Can produce stretches of language with a fairly even tempo; although he or she can be hesitant as when searching for patterns and expressions, there are few noticeably long pauses.	Can initiate discourse, take his or her turn when appropriate and end conversation when he or she needs to, although he or she may not always do this elegantly. Can help the discussion along on familiar ground confirming comprehension, inviting others in, and so on.	Can use a limited number of cohesive devices to link his or her utterances into clear, coherent discourse, although there may be some "jumpiness" in a long contribution.
T+					
T	Has enough language to get by, with sufficient vocabulary to express him or herself with some hesitation and circumlocutions on topics such as family, hobbies and interests, work, travel, and current events.	Uses reasonably accurately a repertoire of frequently used "routines" and patterns associated with more predictable situations.	Can keep going comprehensibly, even though pausing for grammatical and lexical planning and repair is very evident, especially in longer stretches of free production.	Can initiate, maintain and close simple face-to-face conversation on topics that are familiar or of personal interest. Can repeat back part of what someone has said to confirm mutual understanding.	Can link a series of shorter, discrete simple elements into a connected, linear sequence of points.

W+					
W	Uses basic sentence patterns with memorized phrases, groups of a few words, and formulae in order to communicate limited information in simple everyday situations.	Uses some simple structures correctly, but still systematically makes basic mistakes.	Can make him or herself understood in very short utterances, even though pauses, false starts, and reformulation are very evident.	Can ask and answer questions and respond to simple statements. Can indicate when he or she is following but is rarely able to understand enough to keep conversation going of his or her own accord.	Can link groups of words with simple connectors like "and," "but" and "because."
B	Has a very basic repertoire of words and simple phrases related to personal details and particular concrete situations.	Shows only limited control of a few simple grammatical structures and sentence patterns in a memorized repertoire.	Can manage very short, isolated, mainly pre-packaged utterances, with much pausing to search for expressions, to articulate less familiar words, and to repair communication.	Can ask and answer questions about personal details. Can interact in a simple way but communication is totally dependent on repetition, rephrasing, and repair.	Can link words or groups of words with very basic linear connectors like "and" or "then."

APPENDIX E

TEACHER ASSESSMENT CHECKLIST: (DATA COLLECTION INSTRUMENT)

QUESTIONNAIRE W1
The Teacher
Teacher's Name: _____

The Class
Sector: _ Lower Secondary _ Upper Secondary _ Commercial & Professional Schools_ Adult Education_ Other: please specify:

_____

Level of
English Year of English study/Level: _____

The Learner
Name: _____

Sex: M: _ F: _

Mother Tongue: _____ Age: _____

Please rate the learner for each on the 50 items on the questionnaire on the following pages using the following scale. Please cross the appropriate number next to each item:

⓪ This describes a level which is definitely <u>beyond</u> his or her capabilities. Could <u>not</u> be expected to perform like this.

① Could be expected to perform like this provided that circumstances are favorable, for example if he or she has some time to think about what to say, or the interlocutor is tolerant and prepared to help out.

② Could be expected to perform like this without support in normal circumstances.

③ Could be expected to perform like this even in difficult circumstances, for example when in a surprising situation or when talking to a less co-operative interlocutor.

④ This describes a performance which is <u>clearly below</u> his or her level. Could perform better than this.

SPOKEN TASKS							
1.	Can communicate in simple and routine tasks requiring a simple and direct exchange of information.	⓪	①	②		③	④
2.	Can ask for and provide everyday goods and services.	⓪	①	②		③	④
3.	Can make simple purchases by stating what is wanted and asking the price.	⓪	①	②		③	④
4.	Can give and receive information about quantities, numbers, prices etc.	⓪	①	②		③	④
5.	Can indicate time by such phrases as next week, last Friday, in November, three o clock.	⓪	①	②		③	④
6.	Can ask for and give directions referring to a map or plan.	⓪	①	②		③	④
7.	Can buy tickets on public transport using utterances such as "Two returns Central, please".	⓪	①	②		③	④
8.	Can ask for and provide personal information.	⓪	①	②		③	④
9.	Can ask and answer questions about habits and routines.	⓪	①	②		③	④
10.	Can answer simple questions and respond to simple statements in an interview.	⓪	①	②		③	④
11.	Can ask written interview questions he or she has prepared and practised beforehand e.g. about leisure activities, food preferences.	⓪	①	②		③	④

12.	Can initiate, maintain and close simple, restricted face-to-face conversation.	⓪ ① ② ③ ④
13.	Can establish social contact: greetings and farewells; introductions; giving thanks.	⓪ ① ② ③ ④
14.	Can use simple everyday polite forms of greeting and address.	⓪ ① ② ③ ④
15.	Can handle very short social exchanges but is rarely able to understand enough to keep conversation going of his or her own accord.	⓪ ① ② ③ ④
16.	Can express how he feels in simple terms.	⓪ ① ② ③ ④
17.	Can ask for and give or refuse permission.	⓪ ① ② ③ ④
18.	Can make and respond to invitations.	⓪ ① ② ③ ④
19.	Can express or ask for opinions.	⓪ ① ② ③ ④
20.	Can agree and disagree with others.	⓪ ① ② ③ ④
21.	Can use simple descriptive language to make brief statements about and compare objects and possessions:	⓪ ① ② ③ ④
22.	Can use simple language to describe people's appearance.	⓪ ① ② ③ ④
23.	Can explain what he or she likes or dislikes about something.	⓪ ① ② ③ ④
24.	Can describe habits and routines.	⓪ ① ② ③ ④
25.	Can give short, basic descriptions of events and activities.	⓪ ① ② ③ ④

COMPREHENSION						
26.	Can understand what is said clearly, slowly and directly to him or her in simple everyday conversation; can be made to understand, if the speaker can take the trouble.	⓪	①	②	③	④
27.	Native speakers need to make a conscious effort to simplify their language, keeping utterances short, using very restricted, simple vocabulary, speaking slowly and deliberately and sometimes giving exaggerated stress to key words in order for him or her to understand.	⓪	①	②	③	④
28.	Can generally identify the topic of discussion around her which is conducted slowly and clearly.	⓪	①	②	③	④
29.	Needs frequently to ask for repetition, reformulation and the explanation of unfamiliar terms in order to be able to understand.	⓪	①	②	③	④
30.	Can use the situational context to guess meaning.	⓪	①	②	③	④

INTERACTION STRATEGIES

31.	Can use simple techniques to start, maintain, or end a short conversation.	⓪	①	②	③	④
32.	Can invite others into the discussion.	⓪	①	②	③	④
33.	Can ask very simply for repetition when he or she does not understand.	⓪	①	②	③	④
34.	Can ask someone to give more information.	⓪	①	②	③	④
35.	Can consult a dictionary to find phrases which, even if not lexically appropriate, have a good chance of being comprehensible.	⓪	①	②	③	④
36.	Can ask how to say a mother tongue word in the foreign language.	⓪	①	②	③	④
37.	Can identify words which sounds as if they might be "international", and try them.	⓪	①	②	③	④
38.	Can occasionally clarify what s/he means by using simple circumlocutions and extralinguistic means.	⓪	①	②	③	④

QUALITIES OF SPOKEN PERFORMANCE							
39.	Can manage comprehensible phrases with some effort, false starts and repetition.	⓪	①	②	③	④
40.	Can adapt well rehearsed memorised simple phrases to particular circumstances through limited lexical substitution.	⓪	①	②	③	④
41.	Can communicate with memorised phrases, groups of a few words and single expressions and formulae.	⓪	①	②	③	④
42.	Has a sufficient vocabulary for the expression of basic communicative needs.	⓪	①	②	③	④
43.	Shows a limited mastery of a few simple grammatical structures and sentence patterns.	⓪	①	②	③	④
44.	Can link groups of words with simple connectors like "and, "but" and "because".	⓪	①	②	③	④

45.	Has a strong accent, which at times impedes understanding.	⓪	①	②	③	④
46.	Can communicate successfully on basic themes if he or she can ask for help to express what he wants to.	⓪	①	②	③	④

WRITING TASKS

47.	Can write numbers and dates, own name, nationality, address, age, date of birth or arrival in the country, etc., such as on a hotel registration form.	⓪	①	②	③	④
48.	Can write simple notes to friends.	⓪	①	②	③	④
49.	Can write very simple personal letters expressing thanks and apology.	⓪	①	②	③	④
50.	Can add an address, date, title and pre-arranged opening and closing formulae to formal letters.	⓪	①	②	③	④

APPENDIX F

SELF-ASSESSMENT CHECKLIST: FROM DRAFT PORTFOLIO: VANTAGE LEVEL

VANTAGE	1	2

Use this checklist to record what you think you can do (Column 1), and which of the things you cannot yet do that have a high priority for you (Column 2). This checklist has 50 points on it. You and your teacher may wish to add other points relevant to your learning at this level.
 	
    Give yourself one check (√) for things you can do in normal circumstances, and two checks (√√) for things you can do easily. Use one star (*) for things you can't yet do which represent a target for you , and two stars (**) for points with a high priority.
 	
    If you have over 80% of the points checked, you may well have reached *Vantage Level.* Talk to your teacher or look on the Internet page to find out about an assessment that could certify your progress.
 	
If this checklist seems to be aimed too high or too low for you, you will find a slightly higher one (Vantage Plus) and a slightly lower one (Threshold Plus) in the collection on the Internet pages.
	I can do this.
	
	√ = normally
	
	√√ = easily
		I need to learn to do this
		
		* = target
		
		** = priority

Listening		
I can understand in detail what is said to me in the standard spoken language even in a noisy environment.		
I can follow a lecture or talk within my own field, provided the subject matter is familiar and the presentation straightforward and clearly structured.		

I can understand TV documentaries, live interviews, talk shows, plays and the majority of films in standard dialect.		
I can understand the main ideas of propositionally and linguistically complex speech on both concrete and abstract topics delivered in a standard dialect, including technical discussions in his or her field of specialization.		
I can follow main ideas in most conversations between native speakers in which I am not an active participant although I may have difficulty with highly colloquial speech.		
I can use a variety of strategies to achieve comprehension, including listening for main points; checking comprehension by using contextual clues.		
Spoken Interaction		
I can initiate, maintain and end discourse naturally with effective turn-taking.		
I can with some confidence exchange considerable quantities of detailed factual information on matters within my field of interests.		
I can convey degrees of emotion and highlight the personal significance of events and experiences.		
I can engage in extended conversation in a clearly participatory fashion on most general topics.		
I can take an active part in informal discussion in familiar contexts, commenting, a putting point of view clearly, evaluating proposals, and making and responding to hypotheses.		

	I can do this	I need this
I can account for and sustain my opinions in discussion by providing relevant explanations, arguments and comments.		
I can help a discussion along on familiar ground confirming comprehension, inviting others in, and so on.		
I can carry out a prepared interview, checking and confirming information, following up interesting replies.		
Spoken Production		
I can give clear, detailed descriptions on a wide range of subjects related to my field of interests.		
I can understand and summarize orally short extracts from news items, interviews, or documentaries containing opinions, argument, and discussion.		
I can understand and summarize orally the plot and sequence of events in an extract from a film or play.		
I can construct a chain of reasoned argument, linking my ideas logically.		
I can explain a viewpoint on a topical issue giving the advantages and disadvantages of various options.		
I can speculate about causes, consequences, hypothetical situations.		

VANTAGE	I can do this	I need this
Strategies		
I can use standard phrases like "That's a difficult question to answer" to gain time and keep the turn while formulating what to say.		

I can make a note of "favorite mistakes" and consciously monitor speech for them.		
I can generally correct slips and errors if I become conscious of them or if they have led to misunderstandings.		
Language Quality		
I can interact with a degree of fluency and spontaneity that makes regular interaction with native speakers quite possible without imposing strain on either party.		
I can pass on detailed information reliably.		
I can produce stretches of language with a fairly even tempo; although I can be hesitant as I search for patterns and expressions, there are few noticeably long pauses.		
I can communicate with reasonable accuracy and can correct mistakes if they have led to misunderstandings.		

Chapter 3

Exploring the Effectiveness of Self-Assessment Strategies in ESL Placement

Diane Strong-Krause
Brigham Young University

Placing students into appropriate language classes is essential and traditionally accomplished by using some combination of objective exams, essay exams, and oral interviews. However, this approach can be costly in terms of both money and time. It is expensive to develop and print tests, and it takes a great amount of personnel time to administer and grade the tests, particularly speaking and writing tests. An alternative approach is the use of self-assessment questionnaires in combination with, or in place of, these traditional exams.

Self-assessment has several advantages over traditional placement exams. Several years ago, Upshur (1975) suggested that students should be able to respond to questions about their abilities in a language using all their experience with the language, whereas traditional exams simply test a small sample of their language. LeBlanc and Painchaud (1985) proposed that self-assessment is useful for adults because adults generally understand the learning situation they will be in; they also speak a first language, so they understand what is involved in communicating in a language. They also suggested that three other advantages are apparent: (a) less time is involved in completing a self-assessment instrument than with traditional tests; (b) problems with cheating and test security issues are eliminated; and (c) self-assessment involves the students more in making decisions about their education, which increases their responsibility for their own learning.

PREVIOUS RESEARCH ON SELF-ASSESSMENT

Research done in the 1960s and 1970s compared self-assessments with predictors of academic achievement, such as the SAT (Scholastic Aptitude Test) and class grades. In a broad meta study of work undertaken at that time, Shrauger and Osberg (1981) reported that self-ratings seemed to predict academic achievement at least as well as other, more traditional assessments. Few studies, however, focused on using self-assessment of language abilities until the late 1970s and the mid-1980s. Most of these studies involved correlational studies aimed at looking at the relationship between self-assessment ratings and objective exams or teacher ratings. Oskarsson (1978) reports a 1977 study by Balke-Aurell of Swedish students studying English as a foreign language. Correlations between self-assessment and instructors' judgments were .60; the self-assessment and formal tests correlated about .50. In a study of students at the University of Ottawa for placement into French and ESL courses, LeBlanc and Painchaud (1985) found positive correlations (ranging from .39 to .53 on subtests and .53 on total score) between results on a self-assessment instrument and a standardized English proficiency exam. They found the self-assessment instrument placed students just as well as the formal placement test they had been using, with fewer changes in classes being reported using the self-assessment instrument. Janssen-van Dieten (1989) reported similar results in a pilot study assessing grammar and reading skills for students studying Dutch as a second language. Results of the self-assessment instrument correlated between .60 and .79 with the criterion scores; she further indicated that 21 out of 25 of the students would have been placed in the same group if only the SA instrument had been used.

However, other studies focusing on the use of self-assessment instruments have reported conflicting results. In a larger study that included assessment for all language skills (listening, speaking, reading, and writing), Janssen-van Dieten (1989) found little relationship between results of the self-assessment instrument and the proficiency test. Blanche and Merino (1989) found that self-assessments did not correlate with classroom or test performance. Pierce, Swain, and Hart (1993) found very weak correlations between proficiency tests and self-assessment of Grade 8 students in French immersion programs, and in a study focused on how well self-ratings correlated with an English placement exam, Wesche (1993) found "placement via self-assessment was extremely unreliable" (p. 15).

These conflicting results make developing a self-assessment questionnaire difficult for those exploring the possibility of using self-assessment as part of their placement procedures. However, previous studies have described several factors that may have limited the effectiveness of a self-assessment questionnaire, including the wording on the questionnaire, the language skill being assessed, the level of proficiency of the students, the cultural background of the students, and the type of self-assessment task.

One factor that may have affected the results of previous correlational studies is the wording of the questionnaire. Prior research (Bachman & Palmer, 1989) suggested that students found it easier to rate themselves on how difficult they found a task (e.g., How difficult is it for you to read in English?) rather than on their ability to complete a task (e.g., How well do you read in English?).

The level of proficiency of the students may also affect self-assessment ratings. In general, studies report that less proficient students tend to over-estimate their language abilities, whereas more proficient students tend to underestimate their abilities (Heilenman, 1990; Oskarsson, 1984). Heilenman (1990) suggested the reason for this: "The more experience that learners have in a domain, . . . the more likely they are to be aware of the limits of their skills and knowledge" (p. 190).

Another factor appears to depend on which language skill—listening, speaking, reading, or writing—is being assessed. Oskarsson (1984) reported a 1979 study by Rasch which found the ability to assess receptive skills (reading and listening) differed more than the ability to assess productive skills (speaking and writing) and that students were more accurate at estimating speaking than writing. Krausert (1992) also found that students were generally able to self-assess speaking and writing, but not reading ability.

Few studies have focused on how cultural background, or native language background, might affect self-ratings, but there is some evidence (Coombe, 1992) that native language groups tend to assess their language proficiency differently.

In addition, the type of task presented to the student in the instrument may also affect results of self ratings. In general, the literature suggests that tasks asking for global assessments of proficiency (e.g., "How well can you read English?") tend to have lower correlations with scores from objective proficiency instruments than do tasks asking for assessments based on more specific contexts (e.g., "How well can you read a letter in English from a friend describing her apartment?"). Pierce, Swain, and Hart (1993) proposed that "the more specific and focused a self-assessment instrument is, the greater the likelihood that there will be higher correlations with objective measures of proficiency" (p. 39).

PURPOSE OF THE STUDY

It is clear that more research is needed in order to develop effective self-assessment tools and to interpret their results. Few studies have been done on just how specific the instrument should be, and additional research is needed to increase our understanding of how other factors might affect the results of self-assessment questionnaires. The study that follows focused on the following questions:

1. What type of task (or combination of tasks) best predicts placement into language courses?

2. How does gender affect self-assessment ratings? (i.e., Do males rate abilities differently than females?)

3. How does native language background affect self-assessment ratings? (i.e., Do students who speak different languages rate their abilities differently?)

Answers to these questions, along with what has already been reported in the research, will aid test developers in creating self-assessment instruments that make placement procedures for second language programs more efficient.

THE STUDY

The subjects were 81 students attending the Brigham Young University English Language Center (ELC), an intensive English as a second language program. Students in this study spoke Spanish (34), Japanese (22), or Korean (25) as their first language. Thirty-four males and 47 females participated in the study.

The self-assessment questionnaire was first written in English and then translated into Spanish, Korean, and Japanese. The questionnaire consisted of two main parts. The first part included items aimed at getting background information about the students, including name, age, gender, native country, native language, and formal and informal exposure to other languages, especially English. The second part was designed to elicit information about the students' assessment of their English language ability in listening, speaking, reading, and writing.

The entire questionnaire was written in the students' native language (Spanish, Japanese, or Korean) except for the reading and taped listening passages, which were in English. The items were presented from the perspective of the task's difficulty, as suggested by Bachman and Palmer (1989). The questionnaire consisted of four main sections: listening, speaking, reading, and writing. In order to find out which type of task, or combination of tasks, best predicted placement, three types of self-assessment tasks differing in levels of generality were presented in each of the four sections. The first type was a question dealing with a general assessment of ability in English (global task). The second type was an assessment based on 10 descriptions of specific tasks (specific context task). The third type were three actual tasks or, in the case of speaking and writing, detailed descriptions of actual tasks (actual task). Table 3.1 presents examples from the speaking section of the self-assessment questionnaire. (See Appendix A for the complete English version questionnaire.)

Each task type was scored separately, so that each student received three scores in each of the four sections (for a total of 12 scores). Possible scores ranged from 1 to a score to 4 for each of the task types. In the first task, global assessment, a self-assessment rating of A (*It is very hard*) received a 1; a rating of B (*It is hard*) received a 2; a C (*It is quite easy*) received a 3; and a D (*It is easy*) received a 4. For the specific context task, each task description was given a score matching the self-assessment rating, with 1 (*Very Hard*) receiving a 1, 2 (*Hard*) receiving a 2, and so on. These separate scores were totaled and divided by the number of task descriptions assessed, resulting in an average score for this task. In the third task, each of the three actual tasks (or detailed descriptions of actual tasks for speaking and writing) was scored in a way similar to that for the global task. Then these scores were totaled and divided by three for an average score for the actual task part.

TABLE 3.1
Examples From the Speaking Self-Assessment Section

Global Task
Circle the letter of the description that best matches how difficult it is for you to speak English.

A.   It is very hard. I can say some sentences in English about my family and my life, but I can't express difficult ideas in English.

B.   It is hard. I can talk about several subjects and I can tell about an event, but it is still difficult to express some ideas.

C.   It is quite easy. I can express most of my ideas in English, but I still have some trouble with a few words and sometimes I make mistakes in grammar.

D.   It is easy. I can express my ideas about almost anything in English with few mistakes.

*Specific Context**
How difficult would it be for you to do the following in English? Circle the number that best describes what you think.

	Very Hard	Hard	Quite Easy	Easy
Introduce yourself someone else	1	2	3	4
Tell someone about a recent vacation	1	2	3	4

Actual task or detailed task description**

A friend asks you about a recent trip you took. Describe in English what you did. First you went to the mountains for two days where you cooked over a fire and went on several hikes to see some beautiful places. Then you went to a small town with several shops. Although there were many tourists there, it was fun to look in the shop windows. Then you returned home.

Circle the letter of the description that best matches how difficult it would be for you to complete this task.

A.   It would be very hard. I could say a few words, phrases, and maybe a few sentences, but I couldn't talk very long. I could express only some of my ideas.

B.   It would be hard, but I could probably talk for a few minutes. Although I would probably make quite a few mistakes, I could express many of my ideas.

C.   It would be quite easy. I could express my ideas and complete the task, but I would probably make some mistakes.

D.   It would be easy. I could express my ideas and complete the task easily. I probably wouldn't make many mistakes.

*In the questionnaire, there were 10 of these for each skill area.
**In the questionnaire, there were 3 of these for each skill area.

Design and Results

Students completed the self-assessment instrument within 1 week of taking the placement exam, with some completing it before the exam and others after. The traditional placement exam consisted of a 30-minute written essay, a 10–15 minute oral interview, and computer-adaptive exams in reading, listening, and grammar. Based on the results of these exams, students were placed into proficiency levels ranging from 1 (*beginning*) to 6 (*advanced*). Classes in listening/speaking, reading, grammar, and writing were provided at each level.

To determine which type of self-assessment task (or combination of types) best predicted placement scores on the traditional placement exam, stepwise regression analyses were examined for each language skill area (see Table 3.2). A significance level of .05 was used for all statistical tests. The first step in a stepwise regression analysis showed the task that was the best predictor. The second step added the next task that, in combination with the first, was the best predictor, and so forth. The R^2 value for each step indicated the amount of variation in the placement results that could have been accounted for by each task or set of tasks. The higher the R^2 value, the more overlap between the task (or set of tasks) and the placement score.

In every case, the actual task alone (or detailed description of a task for speaking and writing) was the best predictor for placement score. Adding any other task or tasks did not significantly improve the R^2 value. Therefore, the best predictor of placement scores, in general, consisted of ratings on actual tasks (or detailed descriptions of tasks in speaking and writing) in which students rated themselves on how difficult it might be for them to complete the task.

TABLE 3.2

**Summary of Stepwise Regression Analysis
for Self-Assessment Ratings Predicting Placement Scores**

Listening			
Self-Assessment Task Rating	B	SE B	R^2
Step 1			
Actual Task	121.33*	18.93	.36
Step 2			
Actual Task	162.69*	28.70	
Specific Context Task	-66.26	35.01	.39
Step 3			
Actual Task	149.68*	32.82	
Specific Context Task	-76.51*	37.23	
Global Task	25.08	30.45	.39

*$p < .05$.

Speaking			
Self-Assessment Task Rating	B	SE B	R^2
Step 1			
Actual Task	1.05*	0.12	.49
Step 2			
Actual Task	0.95*	0.16	
Global Task	0.13	0.17	.49

Note. The third task did not meet the 0.5 significance level for entry into the model.

*$p < .05$.

| | Reading | | |
Self-Assessment Task Rating	B	SE B	R^2
Step 1			
Actual Task	84.24*	18.80	.20
Step 2			
Actual Task	105.76*	27.23	
Specific Context Task	-30.25	27.71	.22
Step 3			
Actual Task	100.28*	28.05	
Specific Context Task	-50.08	36.39	
Global Task	25.79	30.61	.22

*$p < .05$.

| | Writing | | |
Self-Assessment Task Rating	B	SE B	R2
Step 1			
Actual Task	0.76*	0.12	.36
Step 2			
Actual Task	0.46*	0.19	
Global Task	0.35	0.17	.39
Step 3			
Actual Task	0.57*	0.25	
Global Task	0.38*	0.18	
Specific Context Task	-0.18	0.24	.39

*$p < .05$.

However, further investigation of the R^2 values revealed that the rating on the global task for writing ($R^2 = .34$) alone was almost as good a predictor as the rating on the actual task alone. For the other skill areas this was not the case (see Table 3.3).

To achieve the best results for predicting placement, self-assessment questionnaire developers should design actual tasks for listening and speaking, such as listening to a taped passage or providing detailed descriptions of tasks for speaking. For writing, however, developers could use actual or global tasks. Finally, developers may want to exclude tasks assessing reading comprehension because of the low predictive power ($R^2 = .20$).

TABLE 3.3

R^2 Values of Each Self-Assessment Task
for Listening, Speaking, Reading, and Writing

	R^2		
Skill	*Global*	*Specific Context*	*Actual*
Listening	.22	.12	.36
Speaking	.27	.32	.49
Reading	.09	.06	.20
Writing	.34	.25	.36

In order to determine whether gender or native language background might affect self-assessment ratings, it was necessary to determine whether scores on the traditional placement exam were significantly different between either males and females or among the three language groups. It was possible some group or groups simply began the program with higher language proficiency than the others. Table 3.4 shows the means and standard deviations of placement scores for each skill area by gender and by language group. A two-way multivariate analysis revealed no significant effect for gender [$\Lambda = .982$ $F(4, 71) = .332, p > .05$], for language [$\Lambda = .843$ $F(8, 142) = .157, p > .05$], or for the gender by language interaction [$\Lambda = .964$ $F(8, 142) = .320, p > .05$]. Neither gender nor language group scored significantly higher or lower on the traditional placement exams.

To determine whether gender or native language background might affect how students self-assess their language ability, another multivariate analysis of variance was performed, this time with the self-assessment ratings for each skill area on the actual tasks[1] as the dependent variables. Table 3.5 shows the means and standard deviations for the self-ratings of the actual tasks for each language skill area. The results of this analysis revealed a significant effect for language [$\Lambda = .788, F(8, 140) = 2.21, p < .05$], but no significant effect for gender [$\Lambda = .950$ $F(4,70) = .929, p > .05$] or for the gender by language interaction [$\Lambda = .885$ $F(8, 140) = 1.10, p > .05$]. This indicated no statistically significant difference between how males and females rate their language ability. Gender did not seem to affect self-assessment ratings.

However, it appeared that native language background may have an effect on self-assessment ratings. For more detailed information, a series of one-way ANOVAs were analyzed for each of the skill areas with the self-ratings on the actual tasks for listening, speaking, reading, and writing as dependent variables (see Table 3.6).

---

[1]For the remainder of the study, only the actual test self-assessment ratings were used because this task type was the only viable predictor of all the placement scores.

TABLE 3.4
Summary Table of Means and Standard Deviations of Placement Scores by Gender and Language

	Listening			Speaking			Reading			Writing		
	M	SD	n	M	SD	n	M	SD	n	M	SD	n
Gender												
Male	413	159	33	3.74	1.16	34	559	76	34	3.59	1.1	34
Female	430	152	47	3.87	1.38	47	529	150	47	3.82	1.03	47
Language												
Spanish	411	173	33	4.01	1.14	34	531	108	34	3.93	0.92	34
Japanese	434	142	22	4.05	1.36	22	539	157	22	3.82	0.95	22
Korean	428	143	25	3.53	1.32	25	558	117	25	3.36	1.27	25

TABLE 3.5
Summary Table of Means and Standard Deviations of Self-Ratings of Actual Tasks by Gender and by Language

	Listening			Speaking			Reading			Writing		
	M	SD	n	M	SD	n	M	SD	n	M	SD	n
Gender												
Male	2.51	.81	34	2.48	.81	34	2.91	.63	34	2.18	.83	33
Female	2.49	.78	47	2.58	.88	47	2.90	.72	47	2.30	.75	46
Language												
Spanish	2.84	.77	34	2.88	.74	34	3.06	.59	34	2.56	.74	34
Japanese	2.22	.77	22	2.38	.89	22	2.76	.74	22	1.95	.73	21
Korean	2.28	.66	25	2.21	.82	25	2.83	.73	25	2.07	.74	24

These results showed that for listening, speaking, and writing, there was a significant native language effect on the self-assessment ratings of the actual tasks. At least one of the native language groups rated themselves significantly different from the others in these language skill areas even though there was no statistically significant difference in their mean scores on the traditional placement exams. For reading, however, there was no significant language effect.

TABLE 3.6
Summary Table of ANOVAs With Actual Task Self-Assessment Ratings
of Native Language Groups as Dependent Variables

Source	df	SS	MS	F-Value	P-value
		Listening			
Language	2	6.903	3.451	6.35	.0028*
		Speaking			
Language	2	7.119	3.560	5.50	.0058*
		Reading			
Language	2	1.362	0.681	1.49	.2315
		Writing			
Language	2	5.909	2.955	5.40	.0064*

$*p < .05$.

Although there were some differences in the self-assessment of listening, speaking, and writing, it was not known which group or groups differed or how they differed (i.e., whether they rated themselves lower or higher). Comparisons of the groups using Student-Newman-Keuls procedures revealed that the Spanish-speaking group was significantly different from the Japanese and Korean groups. Inspection of the means for each of these groups shows that although there was no significant difference among their placement scores, the Japanese and Korean speakers consistently rated themselves lower than the Spanish speakers in listening, speaking, and writing.

DISCUSSION

One of the main purposes of this study was to determine which types of tasks on a self-assessment instrument should be used in order to best predict placement into a second language course. The most specific tasks proved to have significant predictive power with the placement exams. This concurs with Pierce, Swain, and Hart (1993), who suggested that the more specific a task, the greater the relationship with more traditional measurements there will be. However, in writing the global rating seemed almost as powerful as the actual task rating in predicting placement.

An examination of R^2 values may help to clarify the meaning of the results. The speaking self-assessment was the best predictor, accounting for almost half of the variance (.49) in placement test scores. The listening and the writing self-assessments had lower R^2 values, each accounting for about 36% of the variance in placement test scores. Reading was the lowest with an R2 value of .20. These findings are consistent with research done by Rasch (cited in Oskarsson, 1985), who found that students could assess their speaking skills more accurately than their writing abilities, and with research done by Krausert (1991), who found that students were able to assess their speaking and writing abilities, but not their reading ability.

The other two research questions dealt with determining whether or not gender or native language background might affect self-assessments. For this study, gender had no effect. Males did not assess their language proficiency differently than females. However, native language background affected the listening, speaking, and writing assessments. Japanese and Korean speakers tended to underestimate their language abilities in these areas. Native language may affect self-ratings. Both of these findings are consistent with the results reported by Coombe (1992).

IMPLICATIONS FOR USING SELF-ASSESSMENT

How can the results of this study be applied for use in language programs? The principle implication is that self-assessment instruments, if developed and used appropriately, may indeed be useful to reduce the costs of placement assessment and at the same time be a viable source of information about a student's language proficiency.

Several guidelines for self-assessment questionnaire developers become apparent from this study. First of all, brief task descriptions did not seem to work well for prediction of placement. Unfortunately, these are commonly used in self-rating instruments, partly because they are relatively short and easy to design. For better results, tasks should be designed that contain more detailed descriptions for speaking and use actual taped passages for listening. Although this adds considerably to the length of the questionnaire, the results should be more useful.

For writing, however, both detailed descriptions and global tasks performed similarly. It would be logical, then, to use a global self-rating task rather than the longer detailed descriptions. Furthermore, self-ratings for reading comprehension should probably be avoided. This study, along with previous research, provides strong evidence that students have difficulty assessing their comprehension of what they read.

For practical purposes, the best instrument design for self-rating would consist of both detailed descriptions of tasks for speaking and a global task for writing. This approach could be cost-effective because both of these skills require the most time and money to rate. The instrument could be used for different purposes. First, it could be sent to students and returned before the students join the program, which would provide some indication of language ability to help in organizing the program. It could also be used for on-site placement to reduce the time needed for testing. The self-ratings could be used in conjunction with other measures such as reading, listening, or grammar tests.

However, the study also suggested that caution should be used when interpreting self-assessment ratings when several language or ethnic groups are involved. Native language background may affect how students rate their language abilities.

Self-assessment can have a place in placement procedures, but many unanswered questions still remain. Further research is needed on self-rating of language ability in the four skill areas, exploring why it is difficult for students to rate their reading comprehension. Also, the effects of native language background on self-ratings using other native language groups should be examined. Finally, further research should focus on how the variation of types and number of actual tasks on self-assessment questionnaires affects the degree to which the self-ratings predict placement into language courses.

APPENDIX A
ENGLISH ABILITY QUESTIONNAIRE

Purpose: The purpose of this questionnaire is to find out about your ability to read, listen, speak, and write in English. There is no one correct answer. The questionnaire will not be graded. Please answer as best you can.

1. What is your name?

2. What is your name in English?

3. What country are you from?

4. What is your native language?

5. Are you male or female? (Circle one.)   M   F

6. How much experience have you had in English? Please describe each major experience below:

When	Length	Description of What You Did

Reading in English

Section 1:

Circle the letter of the description that best matches how difficult it is for you to **read** in English:

A. It is very hard. I can read and understand a few words or phrases in English, but I don't understand most of what I read.

B. It is hard. I can read and understand some parts of what I read, especially if I'm familiar with the topic, but I don't understand all of it.

C. It is quite easy. I generally understand most of what I read although there are still many words I don't know.

D. It is easy. I can read and basically understand everything I read in English.

Section 2:

How difficult would it be for you to **read** the following in English? Circle the number that best describes what you think.

	Very Hard	Hard	Quite Easy	Easy
A 1-paragraph description of what a person looks like	1	2	3	4
A short paragraph about someone's daily activities	1	2	3	4
A 1-page story about a short vacation you took	1	2	3	4
A 3-page magazine article about something you are interested in	1	2	3	4
The international news in a newspaper	1	2	3	4
A 10-page short story	1	2	3	4
A 200-page mystery novel	1	2	3	4
Comics in a newspaper	1	2	3	4
A chapter in a university psychology textbook	1	2	3	4
An article in a professional journal	1	2	3	4

Section 3:

Read the following paragraph. Then choose the description that best describes how difficult it is for you to understand.

Paragraph 1:

Tomorrow John and Mary are going on a vacation. They have saved their money for a whole year so that they can go someplace nice. They have decided to go to an island in the Caribbean. They look forward to enjoying the sun and the beaches during the day. They heard that the water is a beautiful turquoise blue and so clear that you can see the bottom of the ocean. They plan to go scuba diving so they can see the many interesting varieties of tropical fish. At night they plan to go dancing, enjoy good food, and have long, romantic walks on the beach.

Circle the letter of the description that best matches how difficult it is for you to understand this passage.

A. It is very hard. I can read and understand a few words or phrases, but I don't understand most of the passage.

B. It is hard. I can read and understand some parts of the passage, but I don't understand all of it.

C. It is quite easy. I generally understand most of the passage although there are still some words I don't know.

D. It is easy. I can read and understand the entire passage.

Paragraph 2:

It was in January 1982 when I visited the High Tatras for the last time. The High Tatras are mountains in the nation formerly known as Czechoslovakia. This region is one of the last pieces of wild, unspoiled nature in Europe. From the age of 14 I was a member of the mountaineering club, and I used to visit these mountains every month. This visit was my last farewell to the place I loved so deeply, because I knew that the next month I would leave my country forever.

High in the mountains there is a place called "White Fall," where there is a hut used by mountain climbers. I had to walk 8 hours to reach this place. The snow was deep, my rucksack was heavy, and I was alone and tired. The weather was cold and windy, but I had expected it. I examined the hut closely. A couple of years ago there had been a fire and the hut had partly burned up. The roof had a lot of holes, and burned beams hung dangerously in the air. I searched inside for the best place to sleep and prepared my "bed" in one corner which was better protected than the others. It was gloomy inside the hut and I had to strain my eyes, especially when I cooked the soup.

Meanwhile, outside the visibility was getting poorer because of the clouds which appeared in the sky. It was getting colder and the first snowflakes started to fall. Soon the wind changed to a gale and the snowstorm began. I went back to the hut. Snowflakes were whirling even there; rotten beams were creaking and squeaking. I went to sleep afraid, and I dreamed heavy, ugly dreams about avalanches and other disasters.

Circle the letter of the description that best matches how difficult it is for you to understand this passage.

A. It is very hard. I can read and understand a few words or phrases, but I don't understand most of the passage.

B. It is hard. I can read and understand some parts of the passage, but I don't understand all of it.

C. It is quite easy. I generally understand most of the passage although there are still some words I don't know.

D. It is easy. I can read and understand the entire passage.

Paragraph 3:

The idea of bringing groups together to preserve landscapes has been called "cooperative conservation." It links federal, state, local, and private interests. While the idea started with Teddy Roosevelt, preservation efforts quickly became hostile. Not until recently has America returned to this "new" attitude and plan of action. The Nature Conservancy is one environmental group that has worked to save endangered landscapes for many years. The Conservancy manages $20 million in conservation monies each year. They do this by buying land and making certain it is cared for. Today, the Conservancy has a preservation plan called the Last Great Places which targets 28 ecosystems nationwide.

Circle the letter of the description that best matches how difficult it is for you to understand this passage.

A. It is very hard. I can read and understand a few words or phrases, but I don't understand most of the passage.

B. It is hard. I can read and understand some parts of the passage, but I don't understand all of it.

C. It is quite easy. I generally understand most of the passage although there are still some words I don't know.

D. It is easy. I can read and understand the entire passage.

Listening in English

Section 1:

Circle the letter of the description that best matches how difficult it is for you to **understand** spoken English:

A. It is very hard. I can understand a few words or phrases in English, but I don't understand most of what I hear. I like people to talk slowly.

B. It is hard. I can understand some parts of what I hear, especially if I'm familiar with the topic, but I don't understand all of it. Many times I need what I hear repeated.

C. It is quite easy. I generally understand most of what I hear although there are still some words I don't know.

D. It is easy. I can understand basically everything I hear in English.

Section 2:

How difficult would it be for you to **understand** the following in English? Circle the number that best describes what you think.

	Very Hard	Hard	Quite Easy	Easy
Names of colors, family members, hobbies, foods, and other basic vocabulary words	1	2	3	4
Someone introducing one person to another person	1	2	3	4
A student telling about his or her daily schedule	1	2	3	4
Someone describing a recent vacation	1	2	3	4
A short lecture on a familiar topic	1	2	3	4
A dramatic movie	1	2	3	4
An hour TV comedy	1	2	3	4
News on TV or Radio	1	2	3	4
A joke	1	2	3	4
A professor giving a long lecture at a university	1	2	3	4

Section 3:

Listen to the following. Then choose the description that best describes how difficult it is for you to understand.

Listen to Passage 1:

Circle the letter of the description that best matches how difficult it is for you to understand what you heard.

A. It was very hard. I could understand a few words or phrases, but I didn't understand most of what I heard.

B. It was hard. I could understand some parts of what I heard, but I didn't understand all of it.

C. It was quite easy. I generally understood most of what I heard although there were still a few words I didn't know.

D. It was easy. I could understand the entire passage.

Listen to Passage 2:

Circle the letter of the description that best matches how difficult it is for you to understand what you heard.

A. It was very hard. I could understand a few words or phrases, but I didn't understand most of what I heard.

B. It was hard. I could understand some parts of what I heard, but I didn't understand all of it.

C. It was quite easy. I generally understood most of what I heard although there were still a few words I didn't know.

D. It was easy. I could understand the entire passage.

Listen to Passage 3:

Circle the letter of the description that best matches how difficult it is for you to understand what you heard.

A. It was very hard. I could understand a few words or phrases, but I didn't understand most of what I heard.

B. It was hard. I could understand some parts of what I heard, but I didn't understand all of it.

C. It was quite easy. I generally understood most of what I heard although there were still a few words I didn't know.

D. It was easy. I could understand the entire passage.

Speaking in English

Section 1:

Circle the letter of the description that best matches how difficult it is for you to **speak** in English:

A. It is very hard. I can say some sentences in English about my family and my life, but I can't express difficult ideas in English. I need a lot of time to think about what I say.

B. It is hard. I can talk about several subjects and I can tell about an event, but it is still difficult to express some ideas.

C. It is quite easy. I can express most of my ideas in English, but I still have some trouble with a few words and sometimes I make mistakes in grammar.

D. It is easy. I can express my ideas about almost anything in English with few mistakes.

Section 2:

How difficult would it be for you to do the following in English? Circle the number that best describes what you think.

		Very Hard	Hard	Quite Easy	Easy
Introduce yourself or someone else		1	2	3	4
Tell someone about your daily schedule		1	2	3	4
Get to know someone you just met by asking and answering questions		1	2	3	4
Tell someone about a recent vacation		1	2	3	4
Tell someone directions to your home		1	2	3	4
Give a 5-minute talk about your country		1	2	3	4
Tell about your future plans		1	2	3	4
Give a 15–20 minute talk about a familiar topic		1	2	3	4
Give a 50-minute talk about a familiar subject		1	2	3	4
Discuss a controversial issue that you feel strongly about		1	2	3	4

Section 3:

Read the following descriptions of speaking tasks. Then choose the description that best describes how difficult it would be for you to complete each task in English.

Task 1:

A friend introduces you to someone at a party. You talk with each other in English for a few minutes. You tell the person where you are from and why you are studying English. You also tell the person about some of your interests and hobbies. Then you ask the person some questions about his or her hobbies.

Circle the letter of the description that best matches how difficult it would be for you to complete this task.

A. It would be very hard. I could say a few words, phrases, and maybe a few sentences, but I couldn't talk very long. I could express only some of my ideas.

B. It would be hard, but I could probably talk for a few minutes. Although I would probably make quite a few mistakes, I could express many of my ideas.

C. It would be quite easy. I could express my ideas and complete the task, but I would probably make some mistakes.

D. It would be easy. I could express my ideas and complete the task easily. I probably wouldn't make many mistakes.

Task 2:

A friend asks you about a recent trip you took. Describe in English what you did. First you went to the mountains for two days where you cooked over a fire and went on several hikes to see some beautiful places. Then you went to a small town with several shops. Although there were many tourists there, it was fun to look in the shop windows. Then you returned home.

Circle the letter of the description that best matches how difficult it would be for you to complete this task.

A. It would be very hard. I could say a few words, phrases, and maybe a few sentences, but I couldn't talk very long. I could express only some of my ideas.

B. It would be hard, but I could probably talk for a few minutes. Although I would probably make quite a few mistakes, I could express many of my ideas.

C. It would be quite easy. I could express my ideas and complete the task, but I would probably make some mistakes.

D. It would be easy. I could express my ideas and complete the task easily. I probably wouldn't make many mistakes.

Task 3:

You bought an article of clothing at a store, but when you returned home, you found that there was a rip in the material. You must return the article of clothing to the store and describe the problem in English. You take the article of clothing to the store clerk and show him or her the rip. You say you want to return it, but the clerk says that the store doesn't accept returns on clothing. You argue that you haven't even worn it and that you think you should be able to return it. The clerk continues to say that the clothing cannot be returned. You ask to see the supervisor. When the supervisor arrives, you explain what has happened and ask to return the clothing. The supervisor says that the store doesn't accept returns. Then you suggest that you could exchange the article of clothing for something similar. The supervisor agrees to an exchange.

Circle the letter of the description that best matches how difficult it would be for you to complete this task.

A. It would be very hard. I could say a few words, phrases, and maybe a few sentences, but I couldn't talk very long. I could express only some of my ideas.

B. It would be hard, but I could probably talk for a few minutes. Although I would probably make quite a few mistakes, I could express many of my ideas.

C. It would be quite easy. I could express my ideas and complete the task, but I would probably make some mistakes.

D. It would be easy. I could express my ideas and complete the task easily. I probably wouldn't make many mistakes.

Writing in English

Section 1:

Circle the letter of the description that best matches how difficult it is for you to **write** in English:

A. It is very hard. I can write some words, phrases and a few sentences, but it is very difficult to express my ideas in English. I need a lot of time to write.

B. It is hard. I can write one or two short paragraphs about my family, my life, and events, but it is still difficult to express some ideas.

C. It is quite easy. I can write at least one page and can express many of my ideas in English. However, I still have some trouble with a few words and make mistakes in grammar.

D. It is easy. I may make a few mistakes, but I can express my ideas about almost anything in English. I could write 2 or 3 pages in English if I needed to.

Section 2:

How difficult would it be for you to **write** the following in English? Circle the number that best describes what you think.

	Very Hard	*Hard*	*Quite Easy*	*Easy*
A description of you telling your name, age, and where you are from	1	2	3	4
A paragraph about your daily schedule	1	2	3	4
A paragraph describing your house	1	2	3	4
A 1-page paper describing something that happened to you	1	2	3	4
A letter to a friend who only speaks English	1	2	3	4
2 or 3 paragraphs describing your city	1	2	3	4
3 or 4 paragraphs discussing an issue that is very important to you	1	2	3	4
A 3-page paper about your country	1	2	3	4
A 2-page summary of an article you read	1	2	3	4
A 5-page report on an academic topic	1	2	3	4

Section 3:

Read the following descriptions of writing tasks. Then choose the description that best describes how difficult it would be for you to complete each task in English.

Task 1:

You have just moved to study at a new school. Write a letter in English to your friend describing the school and your new schedule.

Circle the letter of the description that best matches how difficult it would be for you to complete this task.

A. It would be very hard. I could write a few words, phrases, and maybe a few sentences, but I couldn't write very much. I could express only some of my ideas.

B. It would be hard, but I could probably write a short paragraph or two. Although I would probably make quite a few mistakes, I could express many of my ideas.

C. It would be quite easy. I could express almost all my ideas and complete the task, but I would probably make several mistakes.

D. It would be easy. I could express my ideas and complete the task easily. I probably wouldn't make many mistakes.

Task 2:

You must write a two-page paper in English describing a frightening experience. You write about an incident when you were a child. You were in a large city with your family when you got separated. You didn't know what to do and were very frightened. You remembered, however, that your parents had told you to stay in the same place where you got lost, so you found a spot to sit down and wait. You were still afraid, but after what seemed an eternity, your family finally found you.

Circle the letter of the description that best matches how difficult it would be for you to complete this task.

A. It would be very hard. I could write a few words, phrases, and maybe a few sentences, but I couldn't write very much. I could express only some of my ideas.

B. It would be hard, but I could probably write a short paragraph or two. Although I would probably make quite a few mistakes, I could express many of my ideas.

C. It would be quite easy. I could express almost all my ideas and complete the task, but I would probably make several mistakes.

D. It would be easy. I could express my ideas and complete the task easily. I probably wouldn't make many mistakes.

Task 3:

You read a 3-page magazine article in your native language about a strange insect that lives in certain jungle areas around the world. Now you must write a summary in English of the article. You tell about where and how the insect lives and describe its life cycle. The main objective of this assignment is to write a summary so clear that someone reading your summary would understand the main points without having to read the original article.

Circle the letter of the description that best matches how difficult it would be for you to complete this task.

A. It would be very hard. I could write a few words, phrases, and maybe a few sentences, but I couldn't write very much. I could express only some of my ideas.

B. It would be hard, but I could probably write a short paragraph or two. Although I would probably make quite a few mistakes, I could express many of my ideas.

C. It would be quite easy. I could express almost all my ideas and complete the task, but I would probably make several mistakes.

D. It would be easy. I could express my ideas and complete the task easily. I probably wouldn't make many mistakes.

Chapter 4

Analyzing Self-Repair:
An Alternative Way of Language Assessment

Erna van Hest
National Institute for Educational Research, The Netherlands

This chapter indicates how the analysis of spontaneous language data, in this case self-repair, can be a helpful instrument for language assessment in the classroom. For this purpose, we discuss the relationship between self-repair behavior and language development and point out the pedagogical value of self-repair data. The discussion is based on the analysis of a large set of self-repair data collected as part of a 4-year project on self-repair (Van Hest, 1996).

The chapter consists of six sections. The first section features a short introduction to the phenomenon of self-repair, dealing with the identification and classification of self-repair and presenting examples of various types of self-repair. The next section provides some background information on the relationship between self-repair and language development. In the third section the research questions and the design of the self-repair project are briefly described. The fourth section presents the results of the data analysis and the section that follows treats the pedagogical implications of self-repair data. The chapter concludes with a short summary of the research results and some recommendations on how to incorporate linguistic data into proficiency testing.

THE PHENOMENON OF SELF-REPAIR

Self-repair data are the corrections or repairs speakers make on their own initiative without the intervention of interlocutors, as opposed to other-initiated repair. Self-repair is the result of the workings of the speech monitor. The monitor can be defined as the speaker's own inspection device, which enables him or her to check the utterance he or she is about to produce, is producing, or has produced. This section first discusses the identification and classification of self-repair, followed by some examples of self-repair.

IDENTIFYING SELF-REPAIRS

An important criterion in the identification of self-repairs is the presence of a clear repair structure, which consists of the following three components:

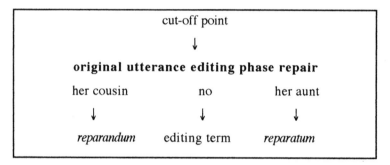

FIG. 4.1: Basic structure of a self-repair.

1. The original utterance containing the so-called *reparandum*, which can be either an error or an inappropriate expression.
2. An editing phase immediately following the moment at which the original utterance is interrupted.
3. The repair proper, containing the so-called *reparatum*, which is the correction or alteration of the troublesome item with or without the repetition of prior material.

When analyzing language learner data for self-repair, it is useful to pay attention to the nonlexical speech signals that may accompany parts of the basic repair structure. Speakers often use signals to accommodate their listeners and to minimize continuation problems. We can distinguish three types of speech signals that can facilitate the identification of self-repair.

One of the most salient speech signals in self-repair is the **cut-off** (^) (i.e., the sudden interruption of the flow of speech), which generally takes the form of a glottal stop. According to Schegloff (1987), a cut-off can function as a "repair initiator" (p. 212). It signals to the listener that what is about to follow may not be a continuation of the preceding utterance, but rather an alteration or correction. As is illustrated in Examples 1 to 4 below, cut-offs can occur at different positions in the original utterance: within the reparandum (1), immediately after the *reparandum* (2), or one or more syllables after the *reparandum* (3 and 4).

1. 'the car is uh is uh ja, uh well is standing uh abo ^ up in the picture'
2. 'it was one of the poems what ^ that was asked'
3. 'the relation between a mother and his son ^ and her son'
4. 'they are just by the ^ they live by the Bible'

A second speech phenomenon that may help to identify self-repair is the so-called "editing term." Editing terms are words like 'uh', 'that is', or 'no' that serve to signal trouble to the listener, while at the same time enabling the speaker to hold the floor and giving him time to plan his repair. They can be defined as filled pauses in the editing phase subsequent to an interruption of the flow of speech and prior or subsequent to repair. Although editing terms are often used to introduce repairs, they are optional elements in the repair structure. Instead of an editing term, there can be an unfilled pause or no pause at all.

A distinction can be made between editing terms with or without semantic value. Editing terms without semantic value such as 'uh' and 'er' are empty fillers, which merely function as discourse markers. Editing terms with semantic value can be described as fillers that are semantically related to the repair under construction. They indicate the kind of linguistic trouble the speaker is experiencing and also help the listener in interpreting the repair. Examples of editing terms with semantic value are 'correction', 'no', 'I mean', and 'sorry'.

5. 'the little girl uh throws a wooden stick uh into the ocean and the dog runs after it, *correction*, it's the uh, uhm cane of the older gentleman'
6. 'he drinks on other people's expenses ^ *no* costs'
7. 'just fourteen ^ thirteen I *mean*'
8. 'I read what I have to write, read *sorry*'

Editing terms are valuable speech signals that facilitate communication. A correct and efficient use of editing terms will add to the (near)-native or native-like character of an second language learner's speech. Moreover, it will certainly influence native speakers' judgments with respect to whether a speaker can be considered fluent.

A third speech signal, the prosodic marking of corrections, can be considered a facilitating cue in the identification of self-repair. A correction is prosodically marked if it is "noticeably different from that of the original utterance" (Levelt & Cutler, 1983, p. 205), for example as a result of an increase or decrease in pitch, loudness, or duration. Through prosodic marking, speakers assign prominence to that element or part of the utterance that is being repaired, in this way signaling the presence of a repair and indicating the semantic relation between *reparandum* and *reparatum*. Very often prosodic marking involves a rejection of the original utterance, as in Examples 9 and 10. By accentuating 'good' in 9 the speaker draws the listener's attention to this part of the utterance and contrasts the *reparatum* 'good' with the *reparandum* 'bad'. The marking of 'niece' in 10 as opposed to 'cousin' has the same contrasting effect.

   9. 'so that didn't go that bad ^ that GOOD'
   10. 'well my cousin, uh no my NIECE'

CLASSIFYING SELF-REPAIR

Once utterances have been checked for possible instances of self-repair, the self-repair selected can be classified according to a list of categories. The two major categories are related to the reasons for self-repair. Roughly speaking, there are two reasons why people can produce self-repair: First, they can correct themselves because they think their utterance is not appropriate enough (so-called "appropriateness repairs"); or second, because they have made an error, (so-called "error-repairs"). Depending on the type of error made, the error-repairs can be divided into phonological (EP-), morphological (EM-), lexical (EL-), or syntactic (ES-) error-repairs. Appropriateness repairs can be further divided into appropriateness lexical repair (AL-repairs) and appropriateness insertion repair (AI-repairs). The following are some examples of self-repair types.

E-Repairs

EP-Repair (Phonological Error Repair) The speaker corrects a phonological error, for example, because of a mispronunciation or an exchange of phonemes.

   11. 'with the g*l*eat ^ the g*r*eat glass elevator'

EM-repair (Morphological Error Repair) The speaker corrects a morphological error, for example, by selecting the wrong ending in the case of verbs or nouns.

12. 'you can choose of lot of *difference*, uhm *different* way for it'

EL-Repair (Lexical Error Repair) The speaker has selected the wrong word and substitutes the correct one for it.

13. 'you must *read* ^ uh *write* the English word'

ES-Repair (Syntactic Error Repair) The speaker produces a grammatical construction that cannot be finished without violating the grammar of the target language.

14. '*it's not you do* ^ *something you do* every day'

A-Repairs

AL-Repair (Appropriateness Repair: Lexical) The speaker replaces one term with another, usually more precise term.

15. 'and then he *is* very sorry ^ he *feels* very sorry'

AI-Repair (Appropriateness Repair: Insertion) The speaker repeats part of the original utterance and inserts one or more words to specify his message.

16. '*a wife* ^ *a thick wife* is uh washing uh the clothes'

Incorrect Repairs

One category of self-repairs that is of special interest in the context of this chapter is the category of incorrect repairs. In these types of self-repairs, speakers replace a grammatically correct utterance with an incorrect one. Examples of incorrect self-repairs are:

17. 'French is *more* beautiful uh *most* beautiful than English'
18. 'last year we *had* ^ we've *had* much more homework'

Whatever the speaker's actual intention, in Examples 17 and 18 he or she clearly did not realize that by replacing 'more beautiful' with 'most beautiful' and 'had' with 'we've had', respectively, he or she produced two grammatically incorrect constructions. Such incorrect repairs are not unusual in language learner data. Most second language speakers are still in the process of learning the language and may, therefore, not yet be aware of all their grammatical mistakes. These incorrect self-repairs can be especially interesting to second language teachers, as they can be an indication of the stage of language acquisition a second language learner is in.

SELF-REPAIR AND LANGUAGE DEVELOPMENT

The identification and the classification of self-repair has been discussed, but how does this relate to the issue of language assessment?

Child self-repair studies with children acquiring an L1 (Clark & Andersen, 1979; Evans, 1985) have indicated that child repair behavior changes over time. Clark and Andersen (1979) carried out a longitudinal study in which they analyzed the spontaneous self-repair produced by 2- to 3-year-olds and 4- to 7-year-olds. They found a relationship between self-repair and age, which was reflected in a shift from simple phonological error repairs, produced by the young children, to the more complex lexical and syntactic error repairs produced by the older children. These data supported their theory that what gets repaired at different stages in the process of language development is related to those aspects of the language the speaker or learner is working on.

Evans' (1985) child repair data supported Clark and Andersen's (1979) conclusions that there was a relationship between age and types of self-repair produced. In addition, Evans (1985) found that older children produced more self-repairs, and repeated and inserted words more often. She suggested that age and self-repair might be related in an inverted U-function: The number of self-repairs first grows with increasing monitoring skills, but then starts decreasing as language skills become more advanced.

Verhoeven (1989) studied developmental changes in second language self-repair. He investigated the use of repeats, restarts, and self-repairs in the spontaneous speech of 74 Turkish children (ages 6 to 8) speaking Dutch as a second language. Verhoeven distinguished between phonological, syntactic, and semantic repairs. His results showed a development similar to that to be found in first language self-repair. With increasing age, there was a decrease in the number of phonological repairs, and, at the same time, an increase in the number of semantic and syntactic repairs.

These and similar studies on the relationship between self-repair and language development (for an overview of studies on L1 and L2 self-repair, see Van Hest et al., 1997) have laid the foundation for a large-scale project on L2 self-repair, the results of which will be discussed in the following section.

THE SELF-REPAIR PROJECT

This section contains the results of a 4-year research project on the L1 and L2 self-repair behavior of three fairly homogeneous groups of Dutch learners of English at three different levels of L2 proficiency. The project included a beginner, an intermediate, and an advanced group of subjects (10 subjects each) who had been learning English for 3, 5, and 7 years, respectively. The subjects were selected on the basis of three criteria: (a) years of tuition in English, (b) school reports and exam grades, and (c) their performance on a test measuring overall language ability (cloze-test and C-test).

The self-repair data were collected by means of two different tasks performed both in Dutch (L1) and in English (L2). The first was a story-telling task. In the field of language acquisition there is a long tradition of using picture story sequences (comic strips) to elicit narrative in the L1 and the L2. This is because story-telling tasks can be easily administered, but, more importantly, they enable researchers to elicit spontaneous speech while controlling the stimulus input and minimizing the influence of dialogic factors such as feedback. In the story-telling task the subjects had to tell 12 picture stories, 6 in Dutch and 6 in English. All of these stories contained one or more humorous reversals and none of them included verbal material. The second task had to be an informal and more natural task, which was to offset the rather controlled and structured format of the first task. The objective was to elicit as much spontaneous speech as possible and, hopefully, many spontaneous self-repairs. For this purpose, an interview task was chosen, which consisted of two separate 20-minute conversations with a native speaker of Dutch and a native speaker of English, respectively.

Approximately 45 hours of L1 and L2 speech production were recorded in all. All tapes were checked for possible instances of self-repair, which were independently transcribed and classified by two trained researchers. In the end about 4,700 self-repair items were analyzed in detail. The results of the data analysis will be discussed in the following section.

Data Analysis

The self-repair project addressed the following questions: (a) Are there any differences between L1 and L2 self-repair? and (b) does L2 self-repair behavior reflect stages of L2 development? In order to answer these questions the self-repair data were analyzed with respect to the numbers of self-repair items produced, the distribution of self-repair items, and the use of editing terms.

The Number of Self-Repairs Produced.   Concerning the number of repairs, the first assumption was that L2 speakers would repair more often than L1 speakers, simply because they make more errors. Earlier self-repair studies by Hieke (1981) and Wiese (1982, 1984) had reported 1.5 to 2.5 times as many self-repairs by L2 as by L1 speakers. In the present self-repair project, 2,079 L1 and 2,623 L2 repairs were collected. These repairs were related to the total number of words per subject in order to obtain the average repair rates. It appeared that, per 100 words, the subjects produced 1.43 repairs in their L1 and 2.28 repairs in their L2, which came down to 1.6 times as many repairs in L2 as in L1. The factor of language proved to be highly significant: $F(1,57)= 24.62$, $p < .001$. These results were in line with Hieke's (1981) and Wiese's (1982, 1984) findings and supported the above hypothesis. Table 4.1 gives an overview of the numbers per language and per level of proficiency.

The second assumption was that the data would reveal proficiency-related differences. The hypothesis was that the beginning L2 learners would produce the most self-repairs, followed by the intermediate and the advanced learners, respectively. Table 4.1 shows that the beginning and the intermediate speakers produced about the same number of self-repairs per 100 words, whereas the advanced speakers produced considerably fewer repairs. A number of statistical analyses applied to examine the relationship between number of L2 repairs and L2 proficiency, revealed significant contrasts between Groups 1 and 3, $F(1,57) = 5.89$, $p < .05$, and between Groups 2 and 3, $F(1,57) = 4.92$, $p < .05$. The contrast between Groups 1 and 2 turned out to be nonsignificant, $F(1,57) = 1.43$, $p < .05$. Apparently both the beginners and the intermediate group were still in the trial and error stage. The advanced group had evidently reached a stage in which language production had become less error-prone.

The Distribution of Self-Repairs. With respect to the types of repairs produced, the hypothesis was, first of all, that in a comparison of the A-repairs and the E-repairs, the relative contribution of E-repairs would be higher in L2 than in L1. The subjects were fluent in their L1, but they were still in the process of acquiring their L2. L2 speakers are very much con-

TABLE 4.1

Average Number of Self-Repairs per 100 Words, per Language, per Level of Proficiency

Level	Dutch	SD	Eng.	SD
Group 1 Beginners	1.70	0.95	2.63	1.05
Group 2 Intermediate	1.35	0.96	2.55	1.21
Group 3 Advanced	1.25	0.87	1.75	1.15
Total over groups	1.43	0.93	2.31	1.19

cerned with the process of language production, especially in the first stages of L2 acquisition. As a result, they are expected to make more E-repairs simply because they make more errors and they are so preoccupied with the linguistic accuracy of the message they want to get across, that they can be expected to pay more attention to errors than to inappropriate words, which are in themselves correct and do not hinder communication.

Second, it was assumed that the L2 learning process of the subjects would be reflected in the types of self-repair that they produced. L1 self-repair studies with developing speakers had reported a shift from simple repairs, such as phonological repairs, to more complex ones, morphological and syntactic repairs, with increasing proficiency. The assumption was that a similar shift in L2 would be found. Depending on the stage of L2 development of the L2 speakers, certain types of errors might be repaired more often than others. Figures 4.2 and 4.3 show the results with respect to the distribution of self-repairs.

The data analyses revealed some clear developments in L2 self-repair behavior. If we take a look at Fig. 4.2 we see that in comparison with the A- and the E-repairs, the relative contribution of E-repairs is significantly higher in

distribution L1 and L2 repairs

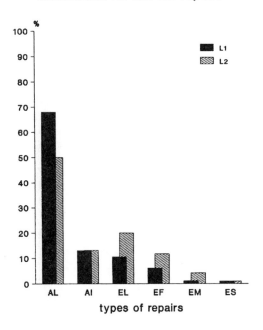

FIG. 4.2: Distribution of L1 and L2 repairs.

L2 than in L1, F (1,27) = 48.82, $p < .001$. So, speakers make more E-repairs in their L2 than in their L1. In addition, the L2 data show (see Fig. 4.3) a significant shift from simple (EP-, EL-repairs) to more complex repairs (AL-repairs) with increasing L2 proficiency, F (1,27) = 7.79, $p < .002$, which confirms the second hypothesis. The effects for language and group are even better illustrated by Figs. 4.4 and 4.5, which show the shifts in relative frequencies for the EL- and the AL-repairs, respectively.

In the case of the EL-repairs first of all we see a clear language effect for Groups 1 (beginners) and 2 (intermediate learners): The beginners and the intermediate learners produce significantly more repairs in L2, F(1,27) = 28.60, $p < .001$ than in L1, F(1,27) = 9.75, $p < .004$. The language effect was absent in the case of the advanced speakers (Group 3).

With respect to effects of group there is a significant contrast in L2 between Groups 1 and 3 and Groups 2 and 3, F(1,27) = 7.88, $p < .009$, and F(1,27) = 3.89, $p < .05$, respectively. The advanced speakers produced significantly fewer EL-repairs (8%) in L2 than either the beginners (13.9%) or the intermediate speakers (12.2%).

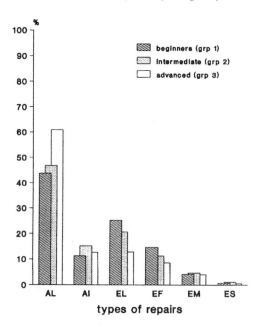

FIG. 4.3: Distribution of L2 repairs per group.

EL-repairs, group and language

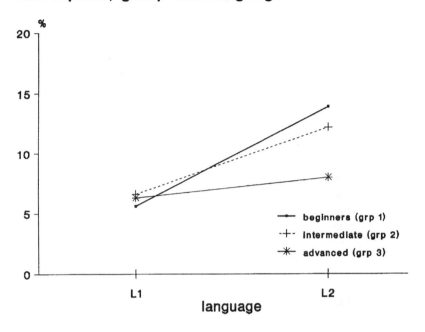

FIG. 4.4: EL-repairs per group and per language.

Figure 4.5 shows a significant language effect for the AL-repairs. Groups 1 and 2 produces significantly more AL-repairs in L1, F(1,27) = 17.22, $p <$ .001, than in L2, F(1,27) = 9.59, $p <$ .005. Group 3 demonstrated the same behavior as in the case of the EL-repairs: Again the language effect for this group was absent.

Just as in the case of the EL-repairs, the AL-repairs demonstrate a significant group effect. Group 3, F(1,27) = 14.72, $p <$ .001, produced more AL-repairs in L2 than Groups 1 and 2, F(1,27) = 7.05, $p <$ .013. This shift in the appropriateness-repair data suggested that the more linguistic skills speakers had available (grammatical knowledge and vocabulary), the better they were able to specify their message. In comparison, the L1 data did not show any significant group differences, which underlined the developmental character of the subjects' L2.

The Use of Editing Terms.   The third type of data that was analyzed was the use of editing terms. The present data show a relationship between the use of editing terms and L2 proficiency level, which is especially reflected in the transfer of editing terms from the L1. The L2 speech of the beginning and in-

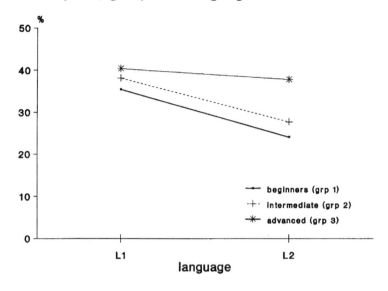

FIG. 4.5: AL-repairs per group and per language.

termediate learners in the project reveals an important transfer of L1 editing terms. This transfer rate drops considerably with the increase of language skills. An analysis of the use of L1 editing terms per subject group showed that the beginning L2 speakers produced 51% of the L1 terms, followed by the intermediate and advanced groups with 38% and 11%, respectively.

IMPLICATIONS FOR LANGUAGE TEACHERS

This section considers the pedagogical implications of self-repair behavior. In other words, how can spontaneous self-repair data be of practical use to language teachers, who are dealing with language learning and language acquisition in the practice of the classroom? First, we discuss the implications in light of the research data. Second, we point out some techniques for elicitation of self-repair data in the classroom.

Pedagogical Implications of Research Data

On the basis of both the present data and earlier self-repair studies we may conclude that there are two aspects of self-repair behavior that can be of special interest to language teachers: the distribution of self-repairs, and the use of editing terms.

The data discussed indicate that self-repair behavior reflects speakers' ability to assess the correctness and appropriateness of the language they produce. What is repaired at different stages appears to be linked to those aspects that language learners have already mastered or are on the verge of mastering. This means that self-repair behavior can provide language teachers with direct and useful information about their learners' level of language competence and about the stage of language acquisition those learners are in. A relatively frequent use of (phonological and morphological) error-repairs will generally suggest that a language learner is in the first stage of language acquisition, whereas the overall presence of appropriateness repairs would be indicative of a more advanced level of language development. By analyzing their learners' self-repairs, language teachers are able to determine what stage their learners are in and to what extent they are aware of language rules and language conventions. For example, incorrect repairs such as Examples 17 and 18 can be very helpful in determining a speaker's level of language proficiency, as they are indicative of the fact that learners have not yet fully mastered the underlying grammatical rules but are clearly trying to work out their correct applications.

The data analysis indicated a rather high percentage of L1 editing terms in the speech of beginning L2 speakers. This percentage dropped with the increase of language skills. A possible explanation for this phenomenon is that beginning learners are so preoccupied with the production process that they can pay little attention to such aspects as the fluency of their speech or the correct use of editing terms. Their first priority is to solve the language problem. Therefore, beginning speakers tend to focus on content words rather than editing terms, which usually carry little meaning. However, as they become more proficient speakers, their speech becomes more automatic and they can spend more time on optional language elements such as editing terms.

So, both the distribution of self-repairs and the use of editing terms are indications of speakers' level of language proficiency. Research data show that advanced language learners distinguish themselves from beginning and intermediate learners by their efficient and strategic use of editing terms and self-repairs. By means of well-planned self-repairs, which give them time to rephrase a structure or to retrieve the appropriate word, they will be able to solve language problems without signaling trouble to their listeners.

Elicitation Techniques

In their analysis of self-repairs, language teachers can limit themselves to the spontaneous self-repairs that language learners produce in the classroom. However, in order to collect some additional self-repair data, teachers can use techniques to elicit self-repair behavior. A direct method is elicitation by means of think-aloud interviews with language learners. These interviews give teachers the possibility to gain insight into the self-repair strategies learners employ while performing a particular task. A less direct method is the use of diaries, in which learners write down the problems they have and the strategies they use in learning a language.

With respect to self-repair behavior in the classroom, it is important that teachers are always conscious of the fact that self-repair is a common phenomenon in everyday speech. If used efficiently, self-repair can be a very functional strategy in communication. Sajavaara (1987) summarizes it as follows: "Learning to speak fluently does not always imply an uninterrupted flow of speech that is sequentially and grammatically irreproachable. The 'good speaker' knows how to hesitate, how to be silent, how to self-correct, how to interrupt and how to complete expressions or leave them unfinished" (p. 62). Unlike language errors, for example, self-repair is not something that language learners should try to avoid as they become more proficient. It is something they should try to develop within the framework of the language they are acquiring.

CONCLUSION

This chapter has shown how results from L2 acquisition data can provide an empirical basis for L2 assessment, and, in particular, how L2 self-repair data can be used as a measure of L2 proficiency. The research results presented indicate a significant relationship between self-repair behavior and level of L2 proficiency. There is an important shift from simple (EP-repairs, EL-repairs) to more complex repairs (AL-repairs) with increasing L2 proficiency and an analysis of the use of editing terms demonstrates some clear changes with increasing level of L2 proficiency. As a result, these language data may be interesting to language testers as well as language teachers in that they provide a linguistic basis for proficiency tests to be geared to the learner's state of development. In this way, self-repair data can be especially useful in formulating descriptors with respect to interaction, oral production, and spoken fluency, as these are all areas that self-repair is inextricably linked to. We hope that the results discussed in this chapter will stimulate similar, alternative approaches in the field of language assessment.

NOTE

An earlier version of this paper was presented at Language Testing Research Colloquium in Tampere, Finland, in 1996.

Chapter 5

Portfolio Practices in Elementary and Secondary Schools: Toward Learner-Directed Assessment

Margo Gottlieb
Illinois Resource Center

There is much latitude in the design and implementation of portfolios. The variety of educational contexts, the diversity of the student population, and numerous instructional approaches all influence a portfolio's portrait. Additionally, at the elementary and secondary school (K–12) levels in the United States, students, teachers, and administrators each have their own perceptions, purposes, and practices with regard to portfolio use. Each stakeholder represents a unique and valuable perspective, and ultimately, is a participant and learner in this dynamic and evolving process. Thus, portfolios are learner-directed.

This chapter examines the theoretical background and practical applications of portfolios. A conceptual scheme for portfolios provides a composite and comprehensive profile of its various dimensions and levels of operation. The framework is then applied to second language learners from linguistically and culturally diverse backgrounds. A research study of educators of these students that reveals their perceptions and reactions to portfolios over a 5-year span follows. The last section explores the promise of portfolios in learner-directed instruction and assessment.

BROADENING THE SCOPE OF PORTFOLIOS

Within the last decade, instructional and assessment practices have tended to merge and blend in K–12 settings. There has been a rise in the legitimacy of performance assessment as a viable expression of students' depth of understanding. Axiomatically, there has been greater reliance on qualitative criteria as descriptors of student performance. The shift away from a strict dependence on standardized, norm-referenced, multiple-choice assessment has resulted in a more reciprocal relationship between teaching and learning and a more balanced relationship between teacher and student.

With assessment becoming more performance-based and classroom-centered, the portfolio has emerged as a personal, multiple-use tool for both teachers and students (Clemmons, Laase, Cooper, Areglado, & Dill, 1993; De Fina, 1992). Portfolios can facilitate collaboration among teachers in defining and judging the contents as well as promoting articulation between teachers across grades. With portfolios, student academic performance can be chronicled in one content area, such as literacy (Farr & Tone, 1994; Smith & Ylvisaker, 1993), across the curriculum and across grade levels (Graves & Sunstein, 1992; Yancey, 1992a). Portfolios can be offered as a learning strategy (Porter & Cleland, 1995), as an opportunity to set and evaluate goals, and as a place for self-reflection.

The purpose and usefulness of the portfolio depend on individual stakeholders (Belanoff & Dickson, 1991). For students, the portfolio can provide accumulated evidence of their cognitive, metacognitive, and social development. For teachers, students' portfolios can showcase what they know, which strategies they use, and how they communicates their understanding. Concurrently, a teacher's portfolio can document teaching effectiveness and professional growth (Seldin, 1991). For administrators, the portfolio can aid in establishing the credibility of a specific service, judging the worth of the general educational program, or expressing a professional voice of leadership (Sunstein, 1992). Finally, for other stakeholders, such as school boards, portfolios can reflect the extent of attainment of broader systemic goals.

Classroom portfolios of the 1990s generally value student input in shaping the contents and making shared decisions based on these contents. This characteristic assumes a developmental stance that recognizes a student's level of reasoning and ability to construct his own intelligence as the backdrop for sound instruction and assessment. The learner-directed orientation of the portfolio can thus be traced to developmental psychology that endorses a more participatory role of students in determining their paths and expressions of learning. This redirection in education to encourage active student involvement has had a direct impact on student assessment, in general, and portfolio assessment, in particular.

DEFINING THE FEATURES OF AN ASSESSMENT PORTFOLIO

The expanding notions and functions of portfolios within the educational and assessment communities call for a more precise definition of the concept. Several features mark an assessment portfolio that distinguish it from other types of portfolios (Gottlieb, 1995). The sum of these attributes represents the minimal requirements necessary to establish an assessment portfolio's validity.

First, an assessment portfolio has a specified purpose that is matched to defined targets with clear-cut criteria. Its purpose is often tied to a decision making function, such as in the case of ESL or bilingual students, determining initial eligibility for a service, reclassifying their status on an annual basis, with eventual transitioning from the service. The purpose guides the direction of the entire assessment cycle, from planning to data collection, analysis, interpretation, and reporting results (TESOL, 1998). In addition, the purpose for assessment dictates the kinds of data that are relevant, useful, and meaningful for the portfolio.

The defined targets within a portfolio can be the instructional intents of a unit of study, course or programmatic outcomes, or specific learning standards. Performance indicators are associated with each of these targets to inform students, teachers, and administrators of the goals that are to be achieved. Instruction and assessment are aligned to these targeted statements and exemplify how, and to what extent, the specified goals are to be attained.

Second, an assessment portfolio is a systematic collection of the processes and products of original work and their associated documentation determined, in part, by student choice. The system for the portfolio reveals the "big picture," that is, the plan for implementation. The plan entails the data points (when and how often data are gathered), the kind of entries (those required and those that are student selected), the range of entries (the types of assessment represented), and the contribution of each entry to the whole. Multiple types of assessment are to be included, rather than reliance on a single approach, in order to ascertain a rich, full description and validation of a student's accomplishments.

Included in the portfolio are direct assessments or the tasks the students perform. Equally important is the choice of rubric, or documentation form, the criteria or descriptors of which serve as a scoring guide for the tasks. The rubric has several important characteristics: It must (a) match the purpose of the task, (b) be aligned with preselected goals or standards, (c) express the full range of student performance, and (d) be openly shared and discussed with students. The task, with its documentation, comprises a performance assessment (Perlman, 1994) that becomes enhanced when coupled with student self-assessment.

Third, the accumulated entries within a portfolio are representative and consistent with a student's performance, growth, or achievement over time. This evidence may be primarily directed at the level of an *individual, classroom, program, school district,* or *state.* It is a stretch to have assessment portfolios operate simultaneously on more than one level. For example, a classroom portfolio that is diagnostic in nature, designed to provide ongoing feedback to students and teachers, is not one likely able to accrue a high enough reliability nor would the information be necessarily useful to serve for district-wide accountability. Therefore, it is critical to identify the level to which the data are to be aggregated, as each serves a distinct purpose and audience.

Portfolios of individual students offer the greatest degree of latitude and flexibility, with numerous opportunities for student input. Those used for classroom assessment are often constrained by group guidelines. However, control and ownership can still ultimately reside with the student. In contrast, portfolios designed for program evaluation often contain a uniform data set that is analyzed at prescribed points in time. Portfolios associated with institutionally important assessment, for purposes of accreditation and accountability, need to be the most rigid and structured in order to establish, maintain, and defend their psychometric properties. Operating at the district and state levels, these portfolios are usually externally imposed on students and teachers with a more limited amount of student involvement.

The primary audiences for portfolios define for whom the information is intended and most useful. At each level of implementation, one group serves as a conduit to the successive one: For example, teachers bridge the classroom to a program, principals link programs to a school or district, and superintendents are the liaison from the district to the state. These stakeholders, by representing a particular rung on the educational ladder, are also generally linked with a prescribed purpose that dictates the kinds of portfolio information available to validate their claims.

This more global perspective of assessment portfolios allows for greater opportunity for reliability and continuity within a designated level, due to a shared vision and experiences on the part of the participants. Additionally, an assessment portfolio firmly grounded at one level has greater potential for applicability and generalizability across levels. Ultimately, it can serve as the bridge between classroom and large-scale assessment (Freedman, 1993).

Given that assessment portfolios can function on numerous levels, with unique purposes and audiences, researchers and practitioners alike need to be aware of the parameters of operation. There are benefits and challenges of using portfolios at each level. For individuals, portfolios are, by definition, student-directed, as students have a voice in their creation and maintenance. Autonomy results when students are offered opportunities to shape and assess the curriculum as well as to select what they consider relevant to their portfolios. These personalized accounts of the learning process motivate and engage students to become responsible learners. One challenge in creating individual portfolios, however, lies in the variation of student personalities and teaching styles. Another negative factor is the lack of previous exposure of students and teachers to an instructional assessment system of this nature; it may prove overwhelming to adjust to this philosophical shift toward student-centeredness.

The portfolio is a contributor to the community spirit of the classroom, as it ultimately is a way of school life for students and teachers. Group decision making is characteristic of classroom portfolios; consensus needs to be reached on many issues, such as the types, numbers, and frequency of entries. Parents are involved as well by being informed of what their children produce, by learning the criteria for evaluation, and by having a chance to react to the contents. Unfortunately, time is a major impediment to portfolio development at the classroom level, as initially there are numerous organizational and management details to which to attend. For example, deciding on a portfolio's physical attributes, determining accessibility and guidelines for use, and ensuring some semblance of comparability across students are some issues to be tackled. Design, modification, or selection of class rubrics to document performance tasks can also be time consuming.

For programs, collaboration and coordination among teachers is key to being able to glean reliable information from portfolios. Articulation across classrooms enables teachers to have a unified instructional and assessment focus and support for student-directed learning. There is also a down side to portfolios at this level of implementation. Requisite to establishing the portfolio's reliability, there must be agreement on programmatic criteria for judging the portfolios. This requirement implies that information from portfolios must be summarized in a standard way prior to aggregation, thus creating another layer of assessment.

For schools and districts, the criterion-referenced, often student-generated, data from portfolios often complement that of standardized, norm-referenced sources. Ideally, irrespective of the approach, all assessment is anchored in the same goals and standards. This consistency facilitates articulation and linkages among classroom and schools. As with the other levels, there are cautions to be noted. First, sustained professional development for teachers, administrators, and the community is necessary to support this effort. Second, provisions must be made to ensure the stability of the portfolio over time, taking into account the mobility of students and teachers.

Finally, for states, portfolio use highlights the value of nontraditional assessment at a time when there still is heavy reliance on traditional forms. An additional benefit at this level is the acknowledgment of the contribution of the portfolio concept to effective schooling. The central concern regarding portfolios involving so many students and teachers is the bureaucracy this initiative creates. Additionally, the usability of the data is questionable, given inherent technical problems, as is its practicality, given the amount of human and fiscal resources expended. Ongoing data collection, analysis, and reporting that occur throughout the academic year are magically reduced to a summative score, thus often negating the original intent.

SELECTING THE DIMENSIONS OF A PORTFOLIO

No matter what the operational level of an assessment portfolio, its technical qualities need to be established. In addition to the features discussed previously, several dimensions define and delineate an assessment portfolio. Three design categories form the basis for dimension selection and validation for the portfolio: overall use, scope and depth, and orientation (see Fig. 5.1). A set of anchor descriptors establishes the range for each dimension. By pinpointing a position on each continuum, stakeholders can create and can, subsequently, defend a portfolio profile.

The determination of the overall use of a portfolio is associated with three dimensions. The first of these relates to its primary function, that is, the extent to which the portfolio is used for evaluation of student work. At the farthest end of the continuum, the portfolio, with established reliability and validity, can substantially contribute to decision making at any level of implementation. At the lowest end, the portfolio remains a collection, often imbalanced in its representation of the curriculum, of benefit only to individual students, parents, and teachers.

The second dimension defines the role of portfolios in assessment: whether it serves to complement other assessment data or whether it is a complete data set unto itself. The third dimension considers the content of

1. OVERALL USE

A.
Data management system	Evaluation system

B.
Supplement assessment efforts	Supplant assessment efforts

C.
Self-reflection	Academic showcase

2. SCOPE AND DEPTH

A.
One curricular area	Extended throughout the curriculum

B.
Representative of one facet of school life	Multi-faceted beyond school life

C.
Single resource	Extensive resources

D.
Single mode of data collection	Multiple modes

3. ORIENTATION

A.
Teacher-directed	Learner-directed

B.
Product	Process

C.
Structured	Flexible

D.
A unit of study	A school career

FIG. 5.1:   Dimensions to consider in portfolio design.

the portfolio; stakeholders need to decide the proportion of social, metacognitive, and cognitive aspects of learning that are to be measured.

The scope and depth of a portfolio, another design category, defines its parameters. The first dimension details the comprehensiveness of subject coverage; from one curricular area—typically writing—to several, to all curricular areas. Next, the contexts for data collection are delineated, from entries limited to classroom work to more multifaceted entries, entailing school and home activities as well as community service. The number of data sources and resources that the portfolio draws upon, such as self, peers, family members, mentors, and teachers, is another determiner of the portfolio's scope and depth. Finally, the number of different modes of data collection, such as audio, video, photographic, and digital forms, shape the portfolio's contents.

The orientation of a portfolio is the last of the design categories. The degree of control and ownership of a portfolio, the first dimension, can reside with a teacher, can be shared between teacher and student, or can be the responsibility of the student with the teacher serving as a mediator and guide. The next dimension, the provision of flexibility, is directly related to the previous one; a teacher-directed portfolio is rather structured whereas a student-directed portfolio has more latitude in selection of entries. A portfolio can be process oriented, restricted to final products, or include any combination of the two elements. Finally, a portfolio can be developed for a specific unit of study and be a month in duration, or as extensive as a lifetime of learning experiences.

Any profile that unfolds from this selection of dimensions is defensible as long as the stakeholders affected have had a voice in the determination of its parameters. However, in addition, it must be congruent with its defined features, match its specified purpose, and relate to its selected level of implementation.

This introduction has set a common understanding and context for portfolio assessment in the K–12 domain throughout the United States. It offers a refined and expanded definition of assessment portfolios that includes multiple perspectives. Five levels of implementation are identified, from individuals to the state, with specified purposes, audiences, and uses. The numerous dimensions of the portfolio shape its form and influence how it is to be utilized. Threaded throughout is the notion that learner-directed portfolios involve the learner in every phase of the development process. Overall, as Arter and Spandel (1992) state:

> Portfolios support the view that assessment should be continuous, capture a rich array of what students know and can do, involve realistic contexts, communicate to students and others what is valued, portray the processes by which work is accomplished, and be integrated with instruction...(A portfo-

lio) must include student participation in the selection of content; the guidelines for selection, the criteria for judging merit, and evidence of student self-reflection. (p. 36)

The remaining sections of the chapter examine the application of portfolios to second language learners in elementary and secondary schools. It further explores the viability of classroom and large-scale assessment portfolios for this student population. A survey of ESL and bilingual education teachers illustrates the changing perceptions of portfolios over time. In the concluding section, there are practical implications of theory and research on portfolios for teachers and administrators.

EXPLORING PORTFOLIO POSSIBILITIES
FOR SECOND LANGUAGE LEARNERS

The value of portfolios for second language students from diverse linguistic and cultural backgrounds is well-documented (Freeman & Freeman, 1992; French, 1992; Fu, 1992; Navarrete, 1990; O'Malley & Pierce, 1996; Pierce & O'Malley, 1992). Portfolios offer these students accessibility to instructional and assessment practices that have historically been restricted to the general education population. Equally important, the students themselves are acknowledged as contributors and the multicultural resources that these students bring to assessment situations serve as rich data sources.

There is a strong rationale for maintaining assessment portfolios for linguistically and culturally diverse students. Traditional, standardized, norm-referenced assessment has never been a reliable or valid indicator of these students' knowledge or performance. When the conceptual framework or blueprint for assessment does not embrace the characteristics of the total student population, or when students have been systematically excluded from the norming population, when demonstration of academic achievement is entirely literacy dependent, gross inequities arise. Yet, the data generated from these assessments often result in high stakes decisions with consequences for the students.

Portfolios designed for second language learners can capture the full range of the students' competencies in one, two, or more languages. By weighing performance in one language in relation to that in a second, students and teachers can glean a sense of a total learner. Developmental portfolios allow students to demonstrate over time their: (a) growth in language proficiency, including oral language and literacy development, (b) conceptual development and academic achievement, (c) language preference and use patterns, (d) attitudinal change associated with acculturation and learning, and (e) acquisition of learning strategies. Irrespective of the developmental area chosen, a portfolio that is student-directed assumes that second language learners have a say in the contents and in the assessment of the contents (O'Malley & Pierce, 1996).

Self-assessment and reflection are the cornerstones of learner-directed assessment; the portfolio serves as the vehicle to facilitate this process (Paulson, Paulson, & Meyer, 1991). Multiple opportunities for self-assessment within instruction allow second language students to develop as independent learners while acquiring English. To promote learner-directed assessment, it is incumbent upon teachers to recognize the necessity for students to have opportunities to express themselves in their preferred language, whether with a partner, in small groups, or independently.

Classroom portfolios recognize individual differences in rates of development, prior educational experiences, and styles of learning. The advantage for second language learners is that portfolios are criterion-referenced; individuals are compared against themselves in relation to an established set of shared criteria and goals. The data amassed in the portfolio, collected as part of ongoing instruction, shape the students' identity through their use of self-reflection and metacognitive strategies. At the same time, the portfolios inform teachers about the effectiveness of their instruction for these students.

There are numerous advantages for maintaining portfolios for second language learners at the classroom level. Student-directed portfolios, in particular, encourage students who have historically been disenfranchised, to: (a) showcase their accomplishments, (b) assume responsibility for their own learning, (c) demonstrate originality and creativity, (d) reason and think critically, (e) make choices, and (f) have a voice in decision making. Classrooms in which portfolio assessment is integrated into the instructional program are generally more student-centered, collaborative, and holistic than classrooms that rely on more traditional forms of assessment (Genesee & Upshur, 1996).

Learner-directed assessment portfolios are the key to a student-centered curriculum. However, at the program and school levels this personalization is diminished. Although some benefits may be retained, the purpose and audience changes and becomes removed from the primary focus, the student. Thus, for second language learners, the portfolio at these levels becomes a mechanism for making programmatic judgements and decisions, such as the effectiveness of ESL or bilingual instruction or the determination of the overall achievement of ESL or bilingual students. As yet, there is little evidence at the state level that large-scale assessment has been designed for linguistically and culturally diverse students, and there are few substantial policies to determine their participation (O'Malley & Pierce, 1994). Nationally, there are six states that reported administering portfolios as part of their nontraditional assessment during the 1994–1995 school year. Five additional states are anticipated to join the ranks (Bond, Braskamp, & van der Ploeg, 1995). Although mathematics and writing portfolios dominate the learning areas, there is a balanced representation of portfolios across the three benchmark clusters: grade levels 2 to 4, 5 to 8, and 9 to 12.

The State Student Assessment Programs Database (1996) reports that 36 states (72%) exempt students who are identified as Limited English Proficient (LEP). Of those for which portfolios are part of their statewide assessment system, California is the sole state that declares that 20% of elementary and 11.5% of high school LEP students are tested. Guskey (1994), in addressing reform efforts in Kentucky, described portfolio assessment's impact on school accountability without ever referencing the demographics of the state. To conclude, in general, states do not use student portfolios for large-scale assessment and, to a large extent, LEP students are exempted from their assessment program all together.

Research on portfolios for second language learning is generally recognized to be practically nonexistent (Herman & Winters, 1994). Portfolio assessment literature, in general, is anecdotal in nature. For example, Tierney, Carter, and Desai (1991) relate information gathered from reading–writing portfolios. Graves and Sunstein (1992) invite teachers, students, and a superintendent to share their stories in painting portfolio portraits. The Arts Propel program (a consortium among Harvard Project Zero, Educational Testing Service, and Pittsburgh public schools) emphasized the role of portfolios in unfolding the processes that underlie long term development in the arts and humanities (Wolf, 1988, 1989). There is no reference on how portfolios influence linguistically cultural diverse students and ESL or bilingual instructional and assessment practices.

INVESTIGATING PORTFOLIO USE WITH ESL
AND BILINGUAL EDUCATORS

In the United States, portfolios have tended to be implemented at the micro and macro levels simultaneously. Examples of top–down educational reform borne through legislation involving portfolios are the programs in Kentucky and Vermont. Concurrently, other initiatives could be described as grassroots or bottom–up, for example, portfolios emerging from classroom practices where teachers use an identified set of instructional strategies, such as in the area of literacy (Batzle, 1992; Farr & Tone, 1994; Frank, 1994; Glazer & Brown, 1993; Murphy & Smith, 1992a). Although Illinois has not been immune from either of these scenarios, having both state-mandated and discretionary assessments at the school or district levels, portfolios have not been part of systemic reform. Many Illinois educators, however, have embraced the notion that students should be more active, engaged learners. As a result, portfolios have surfaced as a means of articulating this educational philosophy.

THE STUDY

Since the 1991 school year, the concept of portfolios for linguistically and culturally diverse students and their teachers has been incorporated into a graduate level assessment course that is one of the requirements for ESL or bilingual approval in Illinois. The class consists of nine 4-hour sessions along with 24 clinical hours devoted to tasks related to the collection and analysis of data from second language learners.

At the close of each quarter, the survey of portfolio use was administered in order to record the participants' perceptions of the practicality and applicability of portfolios to their particular educational settings. This 40-item questionnaire, with internal reliabilities of .97, consisted of a 5-point Likert scale, from 1 (*not at all*) to 5 (*a lot*). For this study, data were gathered during the 1992–1993 academic year; after a 3-year lapse, it was readministered during 1995–1996. The total sample over this period included 258 educators from more than 60 school districts around the state, the vast majority concentrated around the metropolitan Chicago area. The range of experience in the educational field of this group of teachers, tutors, specialists, and administrators spanned three decades.

Measures of central tendency were calculated for the survey items by year. Subsequently, *t* tests were performed on the pairs of data sets (years 1 and 2, years 1 and 5, and years 2 and 5). Overall, results indicated that educators of linguistically and culturally diverse students overwhelmingly acknowledged portfolios as a valuable instructional and assessment tool. The highest ranking item (#30) corresponded to the educators' belief that portfolios exemplify authentic student work. In contrast, the lowest ranking items (#35 and #36) reflected the extent to which educators have actually engaged in portfolio practices for instruction and assessment.

Interestingly, although the decline in usefulness of portfolios for all teachers reaches statistical significance when contrasting year 1 with year 5, the decrease in utility for ESL and bilingual teachers is statistically significant when each of the data points is compared. Similarly, educators reported that portfolios were less useful (at a .05 level) for students at the elementary school level, including those from linguistically and culturally diverse backgrounds.

There were consistently less positive ratings in year 2, with a downward trend readily apparent by year 5. This less optimistic finding at the end of year 5 suggested a general shift in the educators' perceptions of portfolios from being extremely effective tools to a more moderated opinion that portfolios are somewhat useful.

Inspecting Table 5.1, the number of items with statistical significance at the .05 level or greater increases with time, from 15% to 40% to 80% (comparing years 1 and 2, 2 and 5, and 1 and 5, respectively). Interestingly, only one item (#36), the current use of portfolios for assessment purposes, reflects a positive difference between groups; all other items of statistical significance represent a difference in a negative direction. This finding indicates that overall, portfolios have been influential throughout the educational domain, and educators have responded with increased skepticism over time. Ironically, the one exception to this trend is the gaining acceptance of portfolios for assessment purposes.

Between years 1 and 2, the overall use of portfolios became less valued, in statistically significant proportions, by the respondents. In particular, there was a greater negative perception in the ability of portfolios to spark collaboration, communication, or interaction between the teacher and other teachers, parents, and students. Finally, assessment portfolios were pinpointed as having less usefulness than portfolios for other purposes, such as for instruction or data management.

In comparing the survey data from years 2 and 5, other issues in regard to portfolio use appeared to emerge. First, the role of portfolios in instruction for classroom and school level decisions for ESL and bilingual teachers, support staff, and administrators appeared to lessen. In addition, the portfolio's viability in exemplifying a portrait of a student or a developmental chronicle through samples of a student's authentic work, including higher level thinking, attitudes, feelings, and reflections diminished at a statistically significant level as well. Lastly, respondents appeared more skeptical of having opportunities for student input and were less likely to convince others of portfolio advantages.

In inspecting data gathered in the early 1990s compared with that of the mid-1990s, it is important to address the items with the greatest stability over time. Whereas the utility of portfolios across grade clusters maintained a high level of regard, it was most constant for middle and secondary schools. Likewise, the high means for items referring to the purpose of portfolios, as either a repository for background student data or as alternative assessment tool, did not fluctuate over the 5-year period. The use of portfolios for instructional purposes remained unchanged as well.

INTERPRETATION OF RESULTS

By and large, educators exhibited optimism in regard to the potential impact of portfolios on students (including those from linguistically and culturally diverse backgrounds), parents, teachers, and administrators. Interestingly, the only area of growth on the part of educators over the 5-year period was their use of portfolios for assessment purposes. Why? Educators seem to

TABLE 5.1

**Portfolio Use Summary Comparisons Among K–12 Educators:
Years 1 to 2, 2 to 5, and 1 to 5**

Item #	Years 1–2 sig.	Years 2–5 sig.	Years 1–5 sig.
1. Portfolios for: Instruction	.086	.002	.001
2. Assessment	.017	NS	.008
3. Data management	NS	NS	.031
4. Student level decisions	NS	.055	.005
5. Classroom-level decisions	NS	.004	.001
6. Grade-level decisions	NS	NS	.042
7. School-level decisions	NS	.017	.003
8. District-level decisions	NS	.009	.008
9. ESL or Bilingual services	NS	NS	.002
10. Bilingual special education services	NS	NS	.012
11. Language minority students	.082	NS	.001
12. Language majority students	NS	NS	.034
13. Elementary school students	NS	NS	.046
14. Middle school students	NS	NS	NS
15. Secondary school students	NS	NS	NS
16. Mainstream teachers	NS	NS	.004
17. ESL or Bilingual teachers	.027	.017	.001
18. Support staff	NS	.001	.001
19. Administrators	NS	.020	.004
20. Teacher/teacher collaboration	.011	NS	.004
21. Teacher/student interaction	.003	NS	.002
22. Teacher/parent communication	.002	NS	.021
23. Portfolios provide: Reliable data	NS	NS	NS
24. Valid data	NS	NS	NS
25. Background student data	NS	NS	NS
26. Alternative assessment	NS	NS	NS
27. A portrait of the curriculum	NS	NS	.039
28. A portrait of students	NS	.049	.009

continued on next page

29. A chronicle of a student's development	NS	.014	.039
30. Examples of authentic student work	NS	.032	.004
31. Examples of the student learning process	NS	.007	.001
32. Examples of higher level thinking	NS	NS	.002
33. Examples of attitudes, feelings, reflections	NS	.002	.001
34. Opportunities for student input	NS	.001	.026
35. Extent to which: Use portfolios in instruction	NS	NS	NS
36. Use portfolios for assessment	NS	.033	.002
37. Plan to use in instruction	NS	NS	.001*
38. Plan to use for assessment	NS	NS	NS
39. Intend to convince others of portfolio use	NS	.001	.001
40. Value portfolio use	.026	NS	.001

*This item represents a statistically significant increase in the mean rating; all other statistically significant differences are negative.

have a greater understanding of the connection between instruction and assessment. The interest and enthusiasm generated by the students had spilled over to parents and teachers who supported the students' efforts. Portfolios at the classroom level, maintained by students and individual teachers, were able to withstand the rigors of systematic data collection and analysis in order to demonstrate learning in reliable and valid ways.

The initial inflated perceptions of educators as to the blanket usefulness of portfolios appear to have been realistically tamed over time. A multitude of factors can be attributed to this general decline. Contributing influences may include: (a) mixed messages about portfolios at the program, school district, and state levels; (b) not enough opportunities for sustained professional development, collaboration, and networking; and (c) constraints in implementation, in particular, the lack of sufficient time.

Further research on portfolio assessment is desperately needed in order to provide clarification to stakeholders as to their respective roles and contributions to the assessment process. It is important to ascertain, at the individual level, the students' view of portfolios in varying learning environments. That is, in a democratic classroom, how do portfolios stimulate opportunities for negotiation and conferring? How would this kind of classroom climate, which favors peer to peer and student to teacher interaction, for example, influence the acquisition of a second language? In contrast, what are the consequences for students associated with accountability portfolios that are externally imposed? How do the students feel about portfolio assessment and how do they respond to portfolio use? Action research of some of these questions by older students could reinforce self-directed learning.

Likewise, for teachers, investigation could center on the nature of portfolio assessment in varying sociopolitical situations, such as when it is: (a) self-initiated, (b) mandated from a higher level, (c) supported by colleagues, and/or (d) discouraged by the administration. Other issues come to mind as well. How does reliability of individual entries as well as the portfolio as a whole become established and maintained? What is a fair and reasonable set of expectations for second language students who represent a wide range of educational experiences? Action research on the part of teachers could provide tremendous insight into how portfolios are executed at the classroom level.

Research on portfolios is also critical for school and district administrators. Many technical questions could be answered for this group of stakeholders. For instance, how do the results from portfolio assessment correlate with those from standardized, norm-referenced assessment? What are effective approaches to obtain and maintain inter-rater agreement for school or district rubrics? What forms of assistance—professional development, peer coaching, mentoring—best support portfolio assessment?

PURSUING ASSESSMENT PORTFOLIOS: IMPLICATIONS FOR EDUCATORS

Equity for students in elementary and secondary schools can be achieved, in part, through reliable, valid, and fair assessment practices. In the case of an assessment portfolio, that means its purpose is well articulated, its goals outlined, its stakeholders identified, its dimensions defined, its criteria shared, and the learners themselves are part of the process. The integration of the richness and resources of linguistically and culturally diverse students is a critical component of assessment portfolios at every level of implementation.

Portfolios stimulate student interaction with peers and student ownership in the learning process (Genesee & Upshur, 1996). Assessment portfolios allow students to be part of the decision-making process and, based on their goals, help shape their life long learning. Those that promote students' self-reflection extend the boundaries of assessment to include the learner.

Learner-directed assessment, in tandem with portfolio assessment, creates a natural flow of information. The data that are generated are more meaningful than when assessment is conducted in isolation. The added source of information, the student, provides a valuable piece of the assessment puzzle. Decisions about students when made with students, based on comprehensive data from multiple sources, exemplify equitable assessment.

When assessment assumes an advocacy role, such as in the case of ESL and bilingual education, then, for second language learners, the benefits accrued through portfolio use are enabling and facilitate their empowerment

(Cummins, 1989). One way in which teachers' advocacy is realized is through appropriate and challenging instructional and assessment practices. For second language learners, this translates into interactional performance tasks and projects that build on their linguistic, cultural, and educational experiences. Likewise, administrators are to serve as advocates as well. Their understanding of the power structures and the societal implications of assessment, especially for students groups who have historically been marginalized, must be a force in linking the school and district with the community and society as a whole. Assessment portfolios hold promise for all learners, teachers, and administrators.

NOTE

This chapter is based on a paper presented at the Portfolio Symposium at the 18th Annual Language Testing Research Colloquium in Tampere, Finland, August 1996. Thanks go to Sue Rasher, Director, OER Associates, for the data analyses on the study and her contribution to the field of evaluation research.

Chapter 6

Portfolios: Vehicles for Authentic Self-Assessment

Alan Hirvela
Ohio State University

Herbert Pierson
St. John's University

Assessment is best viewed not only as a means of measuring, at a particular point in time, what students know or can do, but also as a process of allowing them to provide a portrait of their own learning through some form of self-assessment. Just as the creative artist knows that the best art may arise from the note that wasn't played or the brush stroke that wasn't made, teachers may best serve students and themselves by knowing when to step back from traditional approaches to assessment and allow for learner-directed assessment. This path of assessment requires two core beliefs: that learners are capable of meaningfully measuring their own learning, and that a viable form of self-assessment exists, especially in such complex domains as language learning and, in particular, writing. For an increasing number of teachers, portfolios are an exciting and appropriate representation of those beliefs. However, it appears that, until now, portfolios have appealed more to the L1 teaching domain—elementary, secondary, and college teachers working with native speakers of English—than to ESL. Although portfolios have been a consistently popular topic at recent TESOL (Teaching of English to Speakers of Other Languages) conferences and other professional gatherings of ESL teachers, there is very little published literature on the use of portfolio assessment in ESL (Hamp-Lyons, 1994).

The primary purpose of this chapter is to add to the ESL practitioners' understanding of portfolios as assessment and self-assessment tools. The chapter treats portfolio assessment in the context of writing instruction and examines the contributions portfolio pedagogy can make toward ESL learners' authentic self-assessment of their efforts and writing achievements in the classroom. This chapter first examines important perspectives on portfolios and assessment and then discusses two university ESL teaching environments where portfolios have been used as both teacher assessment and learner self-assessment tools.

PORTFOLIOS AND ASSESSMENT

Although, as Sommers (1991) observes, "no consensus exists about just what a portfolio is or should be" (p. 154), some common guidelines for their design have emerged. For example, Larson (1991) stated that "portfolios should designate, at least, an ordered compilation of writings" (p. 138). Hamp-Lyons (1991) explained that "a portfolio is a collection of texts the writer has produced over a defined period of time to the specifications of a particular context" (p. 262). Privette (1993) offered the view that "'portfolio' suggests a collection of selected but not necessarily polished or finished pieces. The owner of the portfolio values each of the writings in it for one reason or another" (p. 60). Privette's statement hinted at one of the central features of portfolio pedagogy: learner decision making in the form of choosing items to be included in the portfolio. How much of this learner involvement there is varies from one approach or context to another. However, it is generally believed that learners need to play some role in the construction of their portfolios. As such, as Huot and Williamson (1997) observed, portfolios usually:

> contain not only a collection of student work but also the process of how the writing got to be included in the portfolio. Ideally, students learn to make decisions about their writing in terms of what to include and how to improve what they choose to work on. Portfolios can also contain the reflective work students do as they prepare a body of their work not only to be evaluated but to represent them as writers. In this sense each portfolio can be an individual record of a student's journey to understand herself as a writer. (p. 54)

These comments offer a general view of what portfolios are. Before looking in greater detail at major components of portfolio pedagogy, it is important to understand why the assessment field has experienced a move toward this pedagogy, especially since portfolios, by their very nature as collections of student writing, do not fit within the psychometric parameters assessment practitioners generally prefer.

The notion of portfolio-based assessment began to attract attention around the mid-1980s as a reaction against the psychometric climate prevailing at that time. In the United States in the 1980s, there was growing concern about declining educational standards. This atmosphere led to intense pressure to place more emphasis on testing as a means of raising standards, in accordance with the belief that the more students are tested, the more they will be motivated to improve effort and performance. This demonstrated a lack of confidence in teachers, in that an increased emphasis on testing was expected to make teachers feel more accountable for their own performance and thus improve the quality of their instruction and their commitment to their work. Elbow and Belanoff (1997), in looking back on that period, note that "in retrospect, what was striking was the urgent and growing pressure for assessment, assessment, assessment: test everything and everyone for a score; don't trust teachers" (pp. 22–23). In fields like composition, in particular, this view of learners and teachers was seen as counterproductive to the whole process of teaching and learning the complex, multifaceted skill of writing. As a result, composition specialists began to search for ways of measuring student writing that would be more consistent with the emerging process approach to writing, allowing other views of student writing than single, timed tests, usually placed at the end of a writing course. To cite one example of these early efforts to find an attractive alternative approach to writing assessment, Camp and Levine (1991) explained that:

> Working with researchers from Educational Testing Service, we sought a model of assessment that would build on students' strengths rather than highlight their deficits. Portfolio assessment seemed a most appropriate form of evaluation for our purposes, a test that would be contextualized. (p. 201)

In addition, many composition researchers began to experiment with portfolio-based approaches, and in the late 1980s and early 1990s, these experiments began to receive considerable attention at conferences and in major publications. Of particular importance was a national portfolio conference held at Miami (of Ohio) University in 1992 and influential collections of portfolio papers such as Belanoff and Dickson (1991), Black et al. (1994), Gill (1993), Graves and Sunstein (1992), Smith and Ylvisaker (1993), and Yancey (1992a). Interest in portfolios has reached a point where, according to Callahan (1997), one could say: "Ten years ago few teachers had heard of writing portfolios. Today, however, portfolios are at the center of many discussions of classroom pedagogy, writing assessment, and curriculum design" (p. 295).

Portfolios represent a fundamentally different approach to language assessment, one which enlarges and reshapes the whole notion of what language assessment can and should do. As Murphy (1994a) explained, "Portfolios give us an opportunity to make right some things that have been wrong in assessment. In particular, they offer us the opportunity to make the assessment process a learning process, something very different from the usual assessment scenario" (p. 150). On the one hand, she said, "assessment should teach students something" (p. 151). In addition, portfolios "promise to capture information not easily assessed by other methods" (Murphy, 1997, p. 72). In other words, stated Condon and Hamp-Lyons (1991), "portfolio assessment directly links assessment with instruction" (p. 246).

Portfolio pedagogy emphasizes performative assessment rather than the customary summative assessment found in most testing situations. Whereas, on one hand, disciplines such as mathematics and science may lend themselves to discrete item evaluation of student understanding of formulae, equations, and theories, writing, on the other hand, does not involve discrete points of knowledge. Learners subjectively combine information about writing techniques with their own backgrounds and perspectives as writers and produce texts that are hybrids of acquired knowledge about writing and personal or culturally shaped preferences for writing. Furthermore, writing ability develops gradually over time, and in the process approach now dominant in the writing field, students are allowed extended opportunities through drafts of papers to generate final versions of texts. Assessment, then, must take into account the entire process underlying student performance, and so, says Huot (1994a), "We must challenge the notion that writing is a testable skill or that we can expect students or anyone else to write on demand" (pp. 3–4).

Performative assessment as reflected in a portfolio of student writing covering an extended period of time "emphasizes what the student can do rather than what he/she doesn't know" (Huot, 1994a, p. 3), thereby providing teachers with a more complete understanding of the ability of students to write. Lucas (1992) noted that what is at work in performative assessment is a "formative" view of assessment "where the students' own evaluative activity is allowed to develop" (p. 10). That is, performative assessment, unlike summative assessment, creates room for learner-directed assessment and makes the learner an active and creative participant in the assessment process, rather than an object of it. At the heart of this view of assessment is the belief "that evaluation tools are most useful when they continue over time, when they involve the students in decision making about what and how to evaluate" (Goodman, 1995, p. ix). When we use portfolios, stated Yancey (1992b), "Assessment is seen as a process in which all the parties are bona fide participants, and in which the person whose performance is being assessed is more than an object of someone else's perusal" (p. 18). In short, as Belanoff (1994) noted, "We are forced to face the writer, not just the writing" (p. 23). Unlike other forms of assessment, "when we read a portfolio we get a much stronger sense of contact with the person behind the texts" (Elbow, 1994, p. 53). Given the nature of writing, and certainly that of non-native (ESL) writers, such contact is essential if teachers are to understand better their performance in the writing class. Furthermore, Burnham (cited in Sommers, 1991) stated that the performative nature of the portfolio approach "establishes a writing environment rather than a grading environment in the classroom" (p. 156). At the same time, the learner-directed assessment atmosphere generated by portfolio pedagogy is one in which "students engage in activities that promote learning while becoming more perceptive about that learning" (Smith, 1993, p. 1). Thus, while other forms of assessment attempt only to measure learning, portfolios nurture learning through a self-assessment focus in which learners tell instructors what they have learned or are learning, instead of being told what, according to a score on a test or a timed writing exercise, teachers believe they have learned.

BENEFITS OF PORTFOLIOS

One advantage cited frequently in the portfolio literature is the notion of student authority or ownership caused by the opportunity students have to review their writing and decide (depending on the portfolio approach being used) which pieces they will present to their teachers and/or what they would like teachers to see in that writing. As we discuss later, student reflection on their writing in the preparation of a portfolio is a key concept in portfolio pedagogy and an essential aspect of learner-directed assessment. In such a self-assessment mode, says Dellinger (1993), "This act of choosing introduces the students to the idea that the judgment of what is best is their own" (p. 15). This feeling of ownership is enhanced by the fact that the portfolio experience is not a brief, one-shot presentation of writing. As the portfolio develops over a long period of time and students are given opportunities to reflect on that writing, their sense of authority grows (Ingalls, 1993; McClelland, 1991), a benefit not likely to occur when assessment occurs strictly through teachers assigning grades to individual pieces of writing. A greater sense of authority or ownership can, in turn, increase learner motivation, since learners feel a greater personal stake in the work they produce.

Another often-cited benefit of portfolios is that revision, one of the most important skills taught in the writing class, receives an even richer emphasis. On the one hand, when teachers use a portfolio approach, they create more opportunities for student practice in revision and simultaneously draw greater attention to its importance (White, 1994a). Portfolios also provide teachers with greater insight into student revision skills, especially when, later in a course, students are allowed to select from their portfolio earlier pieces of writing and revise them, incorporating additional knowledge and skills acquired in the course (White, 1996b). Then, too, reflective comments of students on how and why they revised as they did are helpful to them and to teachers (Murphy, 1994a). Also, as Weiser (1994) explained, the emphasis on revision enables students "to put aside, at least temporarily, the paralyzing effect of grades and concentrate instead on improving their writing" (p. 194). Elbow (1994) pointed out that at the same time such portfolio activities take students away from the experience of "writing only as an exercise in being evaluated" (p. 52), they also develop greater appreciation of audiences as they anticipate their reader's reactions while they select and revise pieces of writing.

Other major benefits of the portfolio approach are that "students discover that writing is indeed a form of learning" (Sommers, 1991, p. 154) when they compose explanations (usually in the form of a letter to their instructor that introduces the contents of the portfolio) of what they have included in their portfolio, and why. As they write this introductory letter, they learn about their own writing. Also, because the portfolio has been assembled over a period of time and contains a richer collection of student writing than either individual essays submitted separately or writing exams, teachers may wish to place more grading emphasis on the portfolio. According to Wauters (1991), these higher performance standards will encourage students to engage the portfolio assignment with greater motivation, in the process allowing for more learning to take place while they prepare, with considerable effort, the samples of writing to be submitted to the teacher. Finally, the self-assessment component of portfolio pedagogy will, according to Murphy and Smith (1992b), help students become "active, thoughtful participants in the analysis of their own learning" (p. 58) and in "evaluating their own growth" (Murphy, 1994b, p. 201).

CONCERNS ABOUT PORTFOLIOS

Although portfolios might be seen as alternatives to traditional approaches to writing assessment, in some scenarios that might not be the case. For example, it is not uncommon for universities to require entering freshmen to submit portfolios of high school writing for writing placement purposes. It is also not uncommon for student portfolios to be used as the deciding factor in determining whether they should be allowed to finish a course or a sequence of courses. Then, too, some portfolio approaches make the portfolio either the only or the largest source of a grade in a writing course. In each of these cases, the portfolio may look no different to students than a writing test (Hamp-Lyons, 1994; Hamp-Lyons & Kroll, 1996). Another major area of concern is the complexity involved in grading such collections of writing, such as developing appropriate grading guidelines (Hamp-Lyons & Kroll, 1996), maintaining consistency in portfolio grading (White, 1994a), and avoiding subjectivity in grading (Smith, 1991). Furthermore, in light of such difficulties, questions arise about the validity of portfolio evaluations (White, 1994b). Yet another concern is the lack of research demonstrating conclusively that portfolios are more effective than other forms of writing assessment. As Condon and Hamp-Lyons (1994) noted, "To date, the portfolio has simply been accepted on faith, on writing specialists' *feeling* that the portfolio is better" (p. 277). Huot (1994a) pointed out that "most of the work done with portfolios up to this time has been anecdotal or testimonial, what I call show and tell" (p. 326).

PORTFOLIO APPROACHES

As noted earlier, portfolios may be used for many purposes: as a placement device, where the portfolio helps teachers or administrators decide into which courses students should be placed; as a gate-keeping device, where the portfolio plays at least some role in determining whether students should be permitted to leave a writing course or program, or even to graduate from a school; and as a means of helping evaluate or grade student performance in a specific course. In addition to these evaluative roles for individual teachers, program administrators, and perhaps schools themselves, portfolios are sometimes adopted by entire school districts, and, in a few cases, states (e.g., Kentucky and Vermont) in much larger gate-keeping capacities.

Given this variety of roles, numerous approaches to portfolio pedagogy have emerged in the decade or so since portfolios appeared in the assessment world. The choice of the approach adopted depends on the reasons for which the portfolio will be used. If, for example, the primary purpose is gate-keeping, certain portfolio contents will be necessary to fulfill that purpose.

One of the key questions to answer in determining a portfolio approach is: Who decides what actually goes into the portfolio? Should the teacher or administrator specify contents, or should students be allowed some role in selecting what goes into a portfolio? Another critical question concerns what kinds of materials should be included. Should there be one genre of writing represented, or a variety of genres? For example, should there be only drafts of papers students have written? What about the inclusion of journal entries? And what about allowing later revision of earlier pieces of writing? Furthermore, should students be required to write something (e.g., an introductory letter) explaining what has been included in the portfolio, and why? Should students be required to describe the process by which materials were chosen? A third important question concerns the amount of time and writing the portfolio should reflect. For instance, should the contents represent a student's work during one semester? One academic year? A few years? A fourth central question concerns the basis on which the portfolio contents should be assessed. Should they be based on the quality of the writing included, the progress the writing samples demonstrate, or the effort a student has made? Again, depending on why the portfolio pedagogy is being used in the first place, answers to these questions will vary. However, the consensus seems to be one described by Hamp-Lyons (1991): "The best portfolio assessments collect writing from different points over the course of the year and take into account both growth and excellence" (p. 262).

Portfolio models generally fall within two categories: those that represent the entire body of a student's work or those that include some samples of that work. Terms such as "comprehensive," "formal," and "working" have generally been used to describe portfolios in which students provide all (or a very large portion) of their work over the time period in question. Portfolios involving some of a student's work are often called "exemplary," "selected," "display," or "presentational," to reflect the idea that only representative samples of work have been included.

In the decade or so since portfolio practice began, a wide variety of specific portfolio types has developed. In addition to the most common type of portfolio, one used in a writing course and representing a student's writing efforts in the course, others in the realm of English include a literary portfolio in which students discuss literary texts in various ways (Sommers, 1997), a fiction writing portfolio for creative writing courses (Romano, 1994), and an M.A. in English portfolio containing graduate student work covering their graduate studies (Hain, 1991). Some specialists have envisioned portfolios in other graduate school contexts: one that could be used in many graduate programs (Reynolds, 1994), and one that could be an alternative to the candidacy exams doctoral students must take to qualify for writing a dissertation (Heiges, 1997). Many specialists have described portfolios in disciplines outside English, such as a general science portfolio (Beall, 1994), a biology portfolio (Dorroh, 1993; Gay, 1991), a teaching portfolio (Ekbatani & Pierson, 1998), and a law school portfolio (Dailey, 1997). Graves (1992) discussed a broader based approach involving a "learning portfolio" in which students provide evidence of and analyze their learning in a variety of school contexts. Some practitioners look in the general context of student acquisition of literacy skills. For example, Chiseri-Strater (1992) distinguished between "writing portfolios," "learning portfolios," and "reflective portfolios," in each of which, albeit with different focuses depending on the type, students analyze and present evidence of their literacy development. Johns (1995a, 1995b, 1997) advocated a "student as ethnographer" approach in which undergraduate ESL students compile portfolios investigating the genres of writing used in courses they are taking and displaying their own writing in those genres, especially in their major field of study. Working in a similar vein, Hirvela (1997) described a "disciplinary portfolio" approach in which non-native English-speaking graduate students, also working as ethnographers, discuss what they have learned about the discourse practices in the disciplinary communities they belong to as graduate students. Finally, an entirely different approach and an increasingly popular application of portfolio pedagogy should be noted: teacher portfolios, in which either new or experienced teachers reflect on their own teaching practices.

THE ROLE OF REFLECTION IN PORTFOLIO PEDAGOGY

Yagelski (1997) has recently observed that "one of the tenets to have emerged in the burgeoning literature on portfolios is the importance of self-evaluation" (p. 225). As we have seen in the various perspectives on portfolios discussed earlier, portfolios are an alternative to traditional top–down types of assessment designed by psychometricians and controlled by administrators and teachers. In most portfolio approaches, students play at least some role in the selection of materials appearing in their portfolios. Hence, at the heart of portfolio pedagogy is a place for self-assessment guided by learners. Here is where portfolios are attractive to those interested in learner-directed assessment, especially in the ESL context. As LeBlanc and Painchaud (1985) have pointed out, "It has now become a commonplace belief that to be efficient, a teaching/learning strategy requires that students have some input in their complete learning cycle" (p. 673). Portfolios involving student self-assessment or reflection allow for meaningful input, particularly in the highly subjective and complex domain of writing assessment. As Murphy (1994a) explained, "Portfolios can be used to encourage students to reflect on the pieces they write and on the processes they use to write them. In fact, many teachers who have worked with portfolios consider reflection the single most important learning opportunity that portfolios provide" (p. 147). Portfolios, then, can provide a congenial and significant bridge between assessment and the growing emphasis on self-assessment. There are many benefits arising from the learner-directed assessment common to portfolio pedagogy. Camp and Levine (1991) noted that in a portfolio classroom, "Reflection makes visible much in learning that is otherwise hidden, even from the student writers themselves" (p. 197) as students study the material they have produced in a writing course and decide what to include in their portfolio and how to present it to their reader. A common difficulty for many students, especially L2 writers, is understanding a teacher's responses to their work and learning from those responses. As the Camp and Levine citation suggests, the self-assessment procedures of portfolio pedagogy can enable students to learn from their self-analysis or reflection what otherwise might not have become apparent to them. Students gain a deeper understanding of their performance and abilities as writers, as D'Aoust (1992) pointed out in discussing portfolio-based reflection: "Reflection is the act of pausing to see oneself as a writer. It creates awareness, a sort of self-consciousness about oneself as a writer. It enables a writer to celebrate his or her strengths as well as identify areas to be developed" (p. 43).

Portfolios, said Sunstein (1992), "provide an invitation for self-evaluation. As we reflect on growth, we grow still more" (p. xvi).

In addition to growth, learner-directed assessment situated in portfolio pedagogy changes the entire learning dynamic of the classroom. For example, Dellinger (1993) pointed out that "a reflective learner is an engaged learner. These short pauses to select work for a portfolio increase engagement and motivation and de-emphasize grades" (p. 16). Mills-Courts and Amiran (1991) made a similar observation: "The sort of critical analysis and reflexive thinking which the portfolio requires invites genuine engagement" (p. 108). Furthermore, as Murphy (1994b) noted, "When students are encouraged to make choices and to reflect on those choices, they are encouraged to take responsibility for their own learning" (pp. 190–191). Cumming (1995) noted a related benefit of reflection through portfolios: "Self-evaluation encourages students to take greater control over their own writing skills" (p. 386). In addition, stated Smith (1993), when they reflect in their portfolios, "students engage in activities that promote learning while becoming more perceptive about that learning" (p. 1). All of these benefits—engagement, student responsibility and control over learning, and the promotion of the learning itself—are central to enhanced language learning and writing performance. In discussing portfolios in the ESL context, Gottlieb (1995) asserted that as teachers it is our role "to enhance the students' metacognitive and affective awareness in learning" (p. 1). The learner-directed assessment environment portfolios create offers meaningful opportunities for ESL students to gain such awareness. At the same time, stated Hamp-Lyons (1994):

> Seeing how much progress they have made seems to balance a tendency among many L2 writers to undervalue their own written work. Practice in self-evaluation lets the students realize that "evaluation" means finding what is strong as well as weak, countering the effects of what for many students, L2 and L1, has been a deficit model of response to their writing. (pp. 49–50)

Porter and Cleland (1995) offered this summary of the benefits of reflection accruing from portfolio pedagogy:

1. Reflection allows learners to examine their learning process.
2. Reflection allows learners to take responsibility for their own learning.
3. Reflection allows learners to see "gaps" in their learning.
4. Reflection allows learners to determine strategies that supported their learning.
5. Reflection allows learners to celebrate risk taking and inquiry.
6. Reflection allows learners to set goals for future experiences.
7. Reflection allows learners to see changes and development over time. (pp. 37–50)

It should also be pointed out that it is not only students who benefit from such reflection. Just as importantly, teachers gain invaluable insight into student learning and performance while reading the reflections of their students. Such insight improves our ability to assess students and improves our teaching practices as we examine what students have learned and how they have learned it. Speaking from the teacher's perspective, Romano (1994) said that when he reads student portfolio reflections, "They remove the blindfold from my eyes, and I am a much more efficient, confident, and trustworthy evaluator when I see clearly" (p. 81).

The process of learning to write in a second language is, of course, a complex one. In addition to learning the language itself, students must also learn about the discourse practices and conventions underlying academic literacy in that language. At the same time, as contrastive rhetoricians have shown, they already possess knowledge of the writing conventions of their native language, conventions that may differ considerably from those in English. Hence, our students find themselves in an increasingly complicated world as they move from literacy in their L1 to literacy in their L2. Opportunities for reflection and learner-directed assessment may enable them to better understand their L2 literacy experiences and growth in ways that conventional assessment will not. And, as we have seen, portfolios can be a primary means of facilitating meaningful learner self-assessment of their writing ability. The remainder of this chapter describes two situations in which reflective learner-directed assessment in the form of portfolio pedagogy was practiced in an attempt to enrich student acquisition of ESL writing skills.

PORTFOLIOS IN ESL COMPOSITION AT THE UNIVERSITY LEVEL

International students enrolled in the ESL composition courses at our respective institutions, Ohio State University and St. John's University, have their writing assessed in a number of ways. On a larger program level, they write 1-hour placement exam essays which are used to determine into which of the ESL composition courses they will be placed. Then there is a diagnostic essay they write at the beginning of each course to offer them an additional chance to display their writing ability. Within individual courses, students write papers, journals, and mid-term and final exam essays, with each of these receiving a grade. All exam essays are scored holistically via independent reading by two or three members of the composition staff. In terms of assessment, then, it is possible for instructors to construct an informed view of student writing over a wide range of assessment measures.

However, these means of assessment don't give us a full picture of student competence or performance. They tell us what we think of their work, but they don't tell us what they think. Furthermore, they don't give students a complete picture of themselves as writers. Grades reveal the effectiveness of final products, but they don't account for the processes by which students produced them. Nor do they allow students to reflect on their learning and to form a comprehensive portrait of what they have learned, processes which enrich and bring clarity to the learning experiences of the ESL learner. Thus, there has been a desire on our part to bring students into the assessment process through a form of self-assessment which allows them to reflect on their own learning. Here is where portfolios play an invaluable role.

Our undergraduate writing portfolio is one which, by design, plays an insignificant role in the overall student course grade, but a large role in what happens to them as a course progresses. By keeping the grade value of the portfolio to a bare minimum, we create an environment in which students assemble the portfolio throughout a course not for an external award coming from a teacher, but rather for something more internal within the students. With so little to gain in terms of grades, students feel little incentive to construct artificial comments aimed at receiving a better grade, as might otherwise be the case. This also reduces fears about being penalized by a low grade for not knowing how to approach the portfolio assignment, a very legitimate concern because of the likelihood that assembling a portfolio is a completely new experience to them. Ideally, then, they can engage the portfolio assignment without the pressures and constraints embedded in other writing situations, in a constructive, self-directed frame of mind. The portfolio becomes a more learner-directed, reflexive exercise in which students examine their writing primarily for their own illumination.

At the beginning of a course, students are introduced to the portfolio assignment and told that they will be expected to compile all of their writing as the course progresses. They are also told that at the end of the course, they will submit a display-type portfolio consisting of three self-selected samples of their work: samples reflecting their effort and progress in the course as measured by the students. Samples can be drawn from all of their drafts of out-of-class papers, from their journal entries (usually written in response to assigned readings), from their mid-term exam essay, from in-class writing assignments, and from later revisions of papers written earlier in the course. Normally, students are choosing from among 30 to 40 pieces of writing in all. Near the end of the term they are given a set of portfolio submission guidelines that explain the selection process. Throughout the term they are reminded that they will be asked, through the portfolio, to reflect on their writing. In other words, through the portfolio, a reflexive emphasis is placed on the work they do, and the importance of that reflexivity is pointed out from time to time during the course.

Central to this portfolio pedagogy (and in many such pedagogies) is the mechanism by which students reflect on their writing. This mechanism is a letter written to their course instructor and placed at the beginning of a port-folio folder which contains the three samples of writing. The letter serves as the entry point into the portfolio by identifying its contents and then, in de-tail, explaining why each sample was chosen and what the instructor should look for while perusing the samples. Thus, a student may write something along the lines of "For my portfolio, I've chosen the first draft of my first pa-per, my mid-term essay, and the final draft of my third paper." In the remain-der of the letter, students explain their choices, ideally in considerable detail. These explanations constitute the grist of the portfolio for both stu-dents in terms of their self-learning and for teachers in terms of encounter-ing accounts and perceptions of students as writers.

The value of these introductory or cover letters is emphasized in much of the portfolio literature. This is partly because, as Conway (1994) explained, "It is the cover letter that gets to speak the portfolio's first words, that por-trays the character and the commitment of the writer" (p. 84). In addition, said Condon and Hamp-Lyons (1991), "The cover letter is quite a complex piece of writing in itself. It demands a degree of metacognition, for the stu-dent must write about writing. Thus, the student can show the extent to which the strengths in his or her writing are conscious strengths" (p. 243). Furthermore, as Elbow (1994) pointed out, in the cover letter, "The student must explain and reflect on what is in the portfolio and talk about processes used in writing the pieces and putting the portfolio together. The cover letter helps students become more thoughtful and aware about their writing pro-cesses" (p. 41).

In the cover letter, then, we find the essence of learner-directed assess-ment as students review not only their production in a course but the pro-cesses they engaged in during their various writing experiences. While conducting this review, they learn about their learning, especially as they compare and contrast early and later pieces of writing. Instead of simply comparing the grade for, say, their first paper with the grade for the last pa-per, as they might do under conventional assessment circumstances, in the cover letter generated within the portfolio environment they examine the whys and hows of what transpired between that first and final grade. They take time to pause and look back over the steps they took to move from the first to the last paper and to evaluate on their own terms what they have done. If, for example, they believe the later paper is stronger than the earlier paper, they can discuss what they did as a writer to create the stronger paper. This may (and usually does) entail commenting on weaknesses they see in the earlier paper and the ways they went about correcting those weaknesses. In effect, then, they are examining their learning. Thus, creating an effective cover letter that explores the samples of writing they've selected takes them inside their learning and casts that learning in a newer and more informed light than a mere letter grade would reveal. While discussing their samples, they are measuring their progress and effort in ways the external assessment coming from teachers makes difficult, at best.

In this portfolio pedagogy, then, the cover letter plays the leading role, with a net result described by Reynolds (1994): "The cover letter can tell us so much about the writer that reading the rest of the portfolio contents can seem redundant or unnecessary" (p. 205). In essence, the portfolio cover letter is like the self-portraits created by great artists. A painting of one artist by another artist may be wonderful and highly accurate in terms of capturing the surface features of the artist being painted, but the artist's self-portrait reveals so much more, because he or she is keenly aware of the workings of his or her inner being. In that case, though the self-portrait may not closely resemble the artist as he or she appears physically to others, it will be a far more revealing portrait of that artist. In the same way, a student's grade arising from a teacher's assessment of his or her writing might very accurately reflect the quality of a student's production, but it won't tell us all we would like to know about the learning underlying that production. However valid the teacher-assigned grade, the assessment lacks some authenticity, especially for students, without the insight gained from student input into the assessment. To achieve this fuller degree of authenticity, we turn to a form of learner-directed assessment like the portfolio and its accompanying cover letter.

SAMPLES OF COVER LETTERS

Because the portfolio pedagogy described here is learner-directed and aimed primarily at enhancing student awareness of their own learning and not at assessing their performance or learning, our concern is not the validity or reliability of portfolios as a measure of student writing ability. Instead, we look briefly at the value—mainly to students, but also to teachers—of portfolios in a reflexive rather than assessment mode. What follows, then, is a look at comments made in a few student portfolios, comments that in our experience exemplify the kinds of insight commonly found in several hundred portfolios gathered and examined since the portfolio pedagogy was implemented in ESL composition courses at Ohio State and St. John's University. The sample student comments are from the cover letters that introduce the portfolios.

One of the great values of the portfolio and its accompanying cover letter is what it tells both students and teachers about their composing processes. In the relatively young field of ESL composition, we are still attempting to understand how students writing in a second or foreign language compose in that language. Working much like recall protocols frequently used in composition research, the cover letters often contain detailed and revealing learner-generated descriptions of these processes, descriptions that take us into a student's composing world in ways we might otherwise never experience. Here is one example of such a description in which a student relates how she wrote a paper in response to a literary text:

> Although the first draft of composition #1 is not very good, the sample 2, the final draft of composition #1 can show lots of progress and also many efforts. After the first draft, I started to work on my second draft and then, the final draft. I read the sample essay, the reference materials as well as the story again. When I tried to build my essay, I decided my thesis statement first and wrote three introduction paragraphs based on the same thesis until I felt satisfied with it since a good beginning is very important. Then, I did some planning of my whole essay. When I didn't have ideas about what to write and how to write, I look over some parts or notes I marked when I read the story and the reference materials or sample essays you gave me to stimulate my mind.

Although there are no profound revelations here, we gain valuable insight into this student's behavior as both a writer and a reader. We gain important information about the explorations (the three attempts at the introduction), the planning process (establishing a thesis statement and settling on a satisfactory introduction, then planning the entire paper), and the use of reading (studying reference materials and notes, a sample essay exemplifying how such a paper can be written, and the story itself) which made possible a draft the student felt good about. Indeed, the student's follow-up comments about this second and final draft of the paper also take us meaningfully into the student's writing world and add depth to her comments about her composing process:

> In the long run, I was sure it is really better [than the first draft mentioned at the beginning of the previous quotation]; as you can see in the sample 2, it has good introduction, which follows general to specific principle and thesis statement; it is clearer and shows my two different responses to Rosalie (main character in the story being discussed in the paper). The summary paragraph is also ok. More than that, the most important body paragraph had great development, too. It includes a clear topic sentence, suitable quotations with correct writing method and more explanations. I used lots of examples to support my thesis statement. Additionally, some transitions had been used so the entire essay was connected. Furthermore, I tried to give the reasons systematically in order that reader can get into my ideas easily. Because I did many efforts, I felt great amounts of progress in my final draft. Compared to sample 1, it is much more organized and the content is much more convincing. I also felt more confident to write a response essay and getting used to using quotations and examples.

This learner-directed assessment of the paper adds substance to the previous description of the writer's composing process and demonstrates the student's awareness of writing concepts and meta-language. Just as importantly, we gain a sense of how well the student understood her own progress. She has not simply walked away from the assignment with a judgment of her success based on the letter grade received; by having to reflect on the paper through the portfolio experience, she has been given the opportunity to examine and to appreciate how she made that paper possible. The self-generated understanding gained from this experience may be of benefit to her in future writing situations, since she has now articulated her writing process and has explained the success of that process. That is, the fact of having done so places what she has done in a concrete form that may then be incorporated into her approach to future writing assignments, as opposed to a vague and unexpressed sense of how she writes. Meanwhile, her instructor has also acquired valuable knowledge of writing from the learner's perspective. Such knowledge can be of great benefit in working with other students.

Another portfolio sample further illustrates the useful information about composing processes that emerges from portfolio pedagogy and the cover letter part of that pedagogy. Here the writer is discussing a comparison-contrast paper in which he discussed characters (Rosalie and Zhong Yu) from two short stories:

> Later on, I had to write a comparison-contrast paper. I did not do that before, and at the beginning I tried to arrange my thoughts in my journal, because writing journals is good for me to arrange my papers and I can clear my direction for my main idea. It is one of the advantages that I take from this course and I will keep that as a habit whenever I write a paper. Although the journal doesn't have to be organized I categorized my ideas by dates. On 10/31, I only compared Rosalie's sentimentality and Zhong Yu's silence. On 11/1, I focused on their similar points, and their personalities were pronounced on 11/2. I arranged the differences between Rosalie and Zhong Yu steeply to prepare writing. Of course, I gave a lot of illustrations to support my ideas. After stating the differences between them, I explained the reasons why I think that way and gave some quotations to support my thoughts. Also I added my own suggestions in those journals too. At the end of each journal, I compared their differences and announced who is the best one in that field.

For a writing teacher, this kind of detailed glimpse at the student's writing experience puts the student's performance on an assignment, and in the course itself, in an entirely new light, one that causes delight and provides encouragement when we see that students do not necessarily sit down and mechanically churn out papers. We gain a much richer perspective on what happens with students outside the classroom. However, it is just as helpful for the students to take the time to generate such a portrait of writing, or in this case preparing to write. The process of doing so enables the learner to better understand and appreciate what he or she has done by having to reflect back on and then articulate the components of the composing process.

Simply moving from one writing assignment to the next, and not having the opportunity to reflect on composing processes and writing successes, deprives learners of this invaluable opportunity to reflexively engage and explore their learning. Thus, the addition of a portfolio pedagogy to a writing course allows for more learning to take place as learners study and describe their learning, and their production, while assembling the portfolio.

Let us look now at some other student self-portraits of learning to gain a fuller sense of what learner-directed assessment produces. Note, for example, one student's remark that "In composition #1, the most beautiful thing that I learn is the soul of an essay—a clear thesis statement." To have the student step back from his writing and produce this poetic-sounding reflection helps him by drawing his attention to this particular knowledge and helps teachers by seeing that he has come to this recognition. This same student explained that:

> Today I really understand how to write a "legitimate" essay. To have an introduction, to have a clear thesis statement, to match the thesis statement and the topic sentences, to write a brief summary, to cite relevant and strong examples and to have a conclusion restating the thesis, all of these have never been learned "legitimately" before I come here. Through the writing of composition #1, #2, and #3, I become more confident in writing any kind of essay in future. This improvement I have never expected before.

Having to take the time, courtesy of the portfolio assignment, to think about his learning and to assemble this description of it, leaves this student better positioned to carry what he has learned into other writing situations because he is not simply taking away from the course the factual knowledge of the letter grades he received. Instead, he has reflected on and constructed a detailed and systematic picture of what he has learned, thereby giving that learning structure and substance.

Another interesting, and representative, remark is this one: "I select the Composition #1 because it is my first essay in this class. It is difficult to know how I improve after this class if one does not view my Composition #1." It is encouraging that the student shows real evidence of understanding the value of reflection on learning. He has identified his first paper as a marker from which to view the entire body of his work and his learning, rather than seeing each assignment as an entity unto itself. Furthermore, by establishing this first paper as a benchmark from which to view his later work, he has set up a situation in which he can more effectively pinpoint, and reflect upon, specific areas of improvement as well as steps taken to create that improvement. Such an approach has been very common in our experience of the portfolio pedagogy, that is, students frequently include a very early assignment in their portfolios, accompanied by detailed remarks on why the early writing was not very successful. In more conventional situations, students would have no real reason, many weeks later in a course, to think back to an earlier assignment and to look closely at how they have progressed since then. It may well be that only the grade on the latest assignment will attract their attention. Lost from sight will be the possibly weak or crude efforts early in the course, and, more importantly, full knowledge of how far the student has progressed since that time. How much better it is to have some form of learner-directed assessment in which students can make the kind of statement we just saw and engage in the process of reflection initiated by the selection of early writing as a basis for comparison.

Portfolios do not just help students unravel—for themselves and their readers—what they have learned; they also provide sometimes fascinating descriptions of how students have come to view their learning. One student, for instance, begins the identification of her portfolio samples with the phrase "Three of my achievements over this quarter were…" There is something wonderfully refreshing in seeing a student writing in a second or foreign language viewing her writing as "achievements." They are not simply papers with perhaps high grades; they are achievements borne of her effort and learning. We see a similar moment of excitement in a student's remark that "My last composition for this course was a reward for me. This composition makes me proud of myself." It isn't a grade alone that causes this student's pride; it is the writing itself. Another remark worth noting is a student's comment that "This was when I began to step on the edge of improvement" as she analyzes her second draft of a paper. To see the student recognizing a certain moment in the writing process as a turning point is an experience we are unlikely to have when we, as teachers, are doing all of the assessing. More importantly, our students will not probably have such important experiences. Without some mechanism for reflexivity, our students have little reason and probably no occasion to look back, weeks later, on a writing experience and see its significance in the development of their skills. One final student comment that illustrates these points is this student's lead-in to his discussion of the first sample in his portfolio:

> First, I would like to discuss my Essay #2. I have two favorable reasons for choosing this essay to be my first sample. The first reason is I really love the introduction of the essay, because at that time, I tried to use a special way that I have never exploited before to finish my introduction. If you could see my Essay #1 and Essay #2 at the same time, then you will understand that this is an important improvement for me.

Here we see enthusiasm and pride in this student's account of his writing, and we sense that through the reflexivity provided by the portfolio experience, the student has arrived at a deeper and more significant understanding of himself as a writer in English. It is not just improvement in his writing as reflected in a teacher's grade on the paper in question. More importantly, it is the student's own concrete sense of where he improved and of the fact that the improvement made a difference.

These are only a few samples of many similar remarks made by students as they reflect on their growth and effort as second language writers. In them we see learners looking beyond grades and assessment and into the depths of learning itself. By doing so, they have made that learning more visible for themselves and have also shown their teachers what standard forms of writing assessment cannot: the inner workings of the second language writer. In the second language situation, where learning is not a linear process and progress is not always tangible and indeed may not be amenable to easy or effective assessment by conventional means, portfolios allow learners to take some meaningful control of the assessment experience through a form of self-assessment where the emphasis is on reflection. When they do so, they may walk away from the language learning experience equipped not just with an external assessment of their performance, but more importantly with significant self-awareness and knowledge of their learning. In the long run, establishing for themselves what they have learned may carry more weight and have a longer lasting effect than a mere letter grade can provide. This may be especially true where the grade is not impressive. For example, a student receiving, say, a C+ for a writing course may well be inclined to feel discouraged by such an outcome. However, through a portfolio experience in which the learner reflects on her learning, that C+ can be contextualized in important ways. For instance, the student may have written a very poor first paper, thus practically ensuring a less than stellar grade for the course. Later assignments, however, may show improvement that the final grade doesn't display to others, or to the student herself. By having the time and the means to examine her entire writing experience in the course, this student may produce her own insights into what she gradually came to learn in the course, regardless of what her final grade suggests. Hence, she can leave the course (and enter the next course or other writing situations) with the knowledge that she has strengths as a writer and is on an upward learning curve.

The letters that students are requested to write when they submit their portfolios at the end of the term reveal their own self-assessment of their progress but are also an indication that they are in tune with own personal learning styles. In their letters, they introduce three samples to their instructor, examples that would typically consist of writing done out-of-class, revisions, in-class writing, journal entries, and reactions to in-class or out-of-class readings. These letters of introduction are placed at the beginning of the portfolio and addressed to the instructor. They briefly identify the nature of the writing and explain what it is about each sample that led the student to select it. The letter is graded as part of the assessment of the portfolio, so it is extremely important that students work hard on the letter and that they include many details. The letter and the portfolio provide each and every student with a valuable opportunity to review their effort and progress during the course, and also a time to reflect on the learning styles that brought them to this point. As the students look through all the writing contained in the portfolio, they are able to examine how their skills as writers have changed during the course, as well as how their approach to writing assignments and sometimes their learning styles have changed. Selecting the samples from the portfolio is an important opportunity for students to display the work they feel best about. It is also a chance for students, in their letter of introduction, to freely conduct an evaluation of their writing in the class and talk implicitly or explicitly about their progress.

Although in the beginning students, especially those needing structure and the constant support of the teacher, can be puzzled as to the ultimate purpose of compiling a portfolio and can be even more puzzled when asked to make the selection of three samples and write a letter of introduction, judging from the writing products and the personal insight that has been achieved, this strategy has worked well. There is a consensus among the students who "do the work" and take pride in developing their portfolios that they have learned a lot from the freedom given to them and have acquired personal insight about how they write and under what conditions they do their best work. Below are some typical student testimonials to this fact.

> I perceive that these three composition are my best productions. They were written without any pressure from the environment. And I tried to express myself as good as I could. When you are rushing, you are not able to express yourself because of nervousness and lack of time. I think that these essays are mature and belong to my level.

> I selected these three writings, because I thought the contents of the essays were good, they were well organized, and there was a very little grammar errors since I proofread the drafts. Also, whenever I write something that is related to my experiences and knowledge, a lot of thoughts and ideas just quickly come out of my mind. I can write them in plenty of words. For writing when I get some ideas, I will translate the Chinese words in English, the sentence structures then will be sometimes misunderstood through the translation, because the Chinese sentence structures are totally different with the English sentence structures, so I have to translate them very carefully and specifically.

> I want you to look at my two compositions and journal entries to measure my effort and development as a writer. At first, when I write, I feel free. I don't have any pressure and time limit to do that. I just write down what I saw or feel ... things that came up in my head. Even though I am sure that I make a lot of mistakes on the journal, it is easier to keep writing a journal than to write a composition at the class. I also realize that there are so many things I can write when I

write a journal. It is not only main things, but other small things. For example, what the weather looks like, what kind of atmosphere that restaurant has...etc. When I got upset or when I was upset, I could refresh myself by writing.

CONCLUSION

After nearly 4 years of experience with a portfolio pedagogy, we believe more strongly than ever in the value of portfolio-based reflection for students. Assembling the portfolio and writing the cover letter is one of the final acts students perform in our courses, and our sense is that this experience enables the students to leave the courses armed not just with a letter grade, but with valuable insight into their learning as second language writers. They also depart on a positive note after reflecting on and describing their learning and their achievements. As writing teachers, this is the note on which we most want our students to leave. At the same time, we feel a sense of excitement as we begin reading the portfolios, knowing that we will find accounts of student learning that will often surprise and delight us and will help us know that we have made a contribution to their development as second language writers. Privette's (1993) observation that "each folder revealed a story of a writer growing" (p. 61) reflects our experience as well and confirms the value of the portfolio pedagogy. For us, then, our assessment picture would not be complete, would not have full authenticity, without this important avenue for learner-directed assessment.

Our work with portfolios in two sites confirms for us a point made by Graves (1992): "The portfolio movement promises one of the best opportunities for students to learn how to examine their own work and participate in the entire literacy/learning process" (p. 4). As ESL teachers, and especially as teachers of writing, we feel it is essential for learners to have such opportunities. As Smith (1991) explained, "Portfolios take the testing out of assessment" (p. 282). Knowing how much emphasis our students tend to place on grades and external assessment, and how limited such assessments can be in the complicated realm of second language learning, we need to open ways for students to experience assessment without the often paralyzing or painful experience that conventional assessment measures create. Yancey (1992b) tells us that portfolios are "sensitive to process" and provide an "emphasis on reflection" and an "emphasis on inquiry" (pp. 15–16). In our view, these are important pieces of the assessment puzzle that we must provide for our students in order to make learning, and the assessment of that learning, a richer and more meaningful experience for all involved. D'Aoust's (1992) observation that "portfolios are more than folders; they are a way for writers to meet themselves and shape their writing development" (p. 48) captures the spirit of assessment and learning that we view as vital in today's language teaching and assessment environment.

In this chapter we have shown why, based upon our experiences, some emphasis on learner-directed assessment in the language classroom and especially the writing classroom is a desired approach to assessment. Students can, of course, be asked at the end of a course to fill out self-evaluation forms of their writing. However, a portfolio pedagogy allows for far more reflection and examination than this or similar approaches, and this, in turn, adds authenticity to the self-assessment process.

Work with portfolios shows that they portray student learning in ways from which both students and teachers will benefit, and they add authenticity to the assessment process. The implication for teachers is that portfolios deserve more emphasis in our language teaching and assessment pedagogy. As we develop curricula and course syllabi, we need to leave sufficient room for authentic learner self-assessment to occur.

Chapter 7

Exploring Strategies in Test-Taking:
Fine-Tuning Verbal Reports From Respondents

Andrew D. Cohen
University of Minnesota

Within the last 15 years, verbal reports have been used increasingly as a source of data for determining the strategies employed by learners in their learning and use of second languages, and for describing strategies used in responding to assessment instruments. This chapter first briefly classifies the different types of verbal reports and defines test-taking strategies. Then, ways in which verbal reports have contributed to the understanding of test-taking strategies are discussed. Next, this chapter focuses on problematic issues regarding the methodology itself. Finally, checklists present ways to refine verbal report methods and types of information that should be included in write-ups so that others may better understand the particular verbal report method utilized. Such information would ideally assist researchers in both making comparisons across studies and replicating the study.

CLASSIFYING VERBAL REPORTS

Verbal reports include data that reflect: (a) *self-report*: learners' descriptions of what they do, characterized by generalized statements, in this case, about their test-taking strategies (e.g., "On multiple-choice items, I tend to scan the reading passage for possible surface matches between information in the text and that same information appearing in one of the alternative choices"), (b) *self-observation*: the inspection of specific, not generalized, language behavior, either introspectively (i.e., within 20 seconds of the mental event), or retrospectively (e.g., "What I just did was to skim through the reading passage for possible surface matches between information in the text and that same information appearing in one of the alternative choices"), and (c) *self-revelation*: "think-aloud," stream-of-consciousness disclosure of thought processes while the information is being attended to (e.g., "Hmm. I wonder if the information in one of these alternative choices also appears in the text"). Verbal reports can, and usually do, comprise some combination of these (Cohen, 1987; Cohen & Hosenfeld, 1981; Radford, 1974).

Questionnaires and other kinds of prompts that ask learners to describe the way they usually take a certain type of language test are likely to elicit self-report data. Self-observation data would entail reference to some actual instances of language testing behavior. For example, entries in journals or diaries that retrospectively describe some language testing event involving the subjunctive would count as retrospective self-observation. Self-revelation or think-aloud data are only available at the time that the language event is taking place, and the assumption would be that the respondent is simply describing, say, the struggle to use the correct form of the subject in an oral or written language task, and not attempting to analyze this struggle. Thoughts that are immediately analyzed would constitute introspective self-observation—for example, "Now, does this utterance call for the present or imperfect subjunctive? Let me see..."

Examples in the second-language strategy literature (not specific to language test-taking strategies) where verbal reports have consisted of self-report interviews and questionnaires include Naiman, Fröhlich, Stern, and Todesco (1978), O'Malley, Chamot, Stewner-Manzanares, Kupper, and Russo (1985), Wenden (1985), Ramírez (1986), and Oxford, Nyikos, and Crookall (1987). In the studies referred to in this literature, the respondents answered interview questions or completed written questionnaires about their language learning and use strategies. Because self-reports have been shown to be somewhat removed from the cognitive events being described, this approach may produce data that are of questionable validity. Questionnaire items are more likely to elicit learners' beliefs about what they do, rather than what they actually do. Efforts are often made by investigators to increase the extent of self-observational and self-revelational data and decrease the amount of self-reports. The purpose is to obtain data that describe the learning event at or near the moment it occurs. Such data might be expected to more accurately reflect what learners actually do than might the response to a questionnaire item calling for a description of generalized behavior.

The reason why verbal reports have gained popularity in the last several decades, despite frequent criticism (e.g., see Afflerbach & Johnston, 1984; Olson, Duffy, & Mack, 1984; Lyons, 1986; Seliger, 1983) is that this research methodology provides data on cognitive processes and learner responses that otherwise would have to be investigated only indirectly. Furthermore, verbal reports have at times provided access to the reasoning processes underlying cognition, response, and decision making. A major impetus for the use of this research technique in second language acquisition and assessment has been its successful use in first-language studies, especially in research on cognitive processes in first-language reading and writing (e.g., Flower & Hayes, 1984; Garner, 1982).

WHAT IS MEANT BY TEST-TAKING STRATEGIES?

Test-taking strategies are defined as those test-taking processes that the respondents have selected and that they are conscious of, at least to some degree. In other words, the notion of strategy implies an element of selection. Otherwise, the processes would not be considered as strategies. At times, these strategies constitute opting out of the language task at hand (e.g., through a surface matching of identical information in the passage and in one of the response choices). At other times, the strategies may constitute shortcuts to arriving at answers (e.g., not reading the text as instructed but simply looking immediately for the answers to the given reading comprehension questions). In such cases, the respondents may be using *test-wiseness*[1] to circumvent the need to tap their actual language knowledge or lack of it, consistent with Franson's (1984) assertion that respondents may not proceed via the text but rather around it. In the majority of testing situations, however, test-taking strategies do not lead to opting out or to the use of short cuts. In some cases, quite the contrary holds true. One Hebrew second-language respondent in a study of test-taking strategies in Israel determined that he had to produce a written translation of a text before he could respond to questions dealing with that text (Cohen & Aphek, 1979).

At times, the use of a limited number of strategies in a response to an item may indicate genuine control over the item, assuming that these strategies are well-chosen and are used effectively. At other times, true control requires the use of a host of strategies. It is also best not to assume that any test-taking strategy is a good or a poor choice for a given task. It depends on how given test-takers—with their particular cognitive style profile and degree of cognitive flexibility, their language knowledge, and their repertoire of test-taking strategies—employ these strategies at a given moment on a given task. Some respondents may get by with the use of a limited number of

---

[1]Allan (1992) developed a test of test-wiseness for ESL students. The test included stem-option cues, in which it was possible to match information from the stem with information in the correct option; grammatical cues, where only one alternative matched the stem grammatically; similar options, where several distractors could be eliminated because they essentially said the same thing; and item giveaways, where another item already gave away the information.

strategies that they use well for the most part. Others may be aware of an extensive number of strategies but may use few, if any, of them effectively. For example, while a particular skimming strategy (such as paying attention to subheadings) may provide adequate preparation for a given test-taker on a recall task, the same strategy may not work well for another respondent. It also may not work well for the same respondent on another text which lacks reader-friendly subheadings.

The ability of learners to use language strategies has been referred to as their *strategic competence,* a component of communicative language use (Canale & Swain, 1980). This model puts the emphasis on *compensatory* strategies, that is, strategies used to compensate or remediate for a lack in some language area. When put on the spot, respondents may omit material because they do not know it, or produce different material from what they would like to with the hope that it will be acceptable in the given context. They may use lexical avoidance, simplification, or approximation when the exact word escapes them under the pressure of the test or because they simply do not know the word well or at all.

Bachman (1990) provided a broader theoretical model for viewing strategic competence, and then Bachman and Palmer (1996) refined the Bachman (1990) categories somewhat. The current framework includes an *assessment* component, whereby the respondents (in our case of language testing) assess which communicative goals are achievable and what linguistic resources are needed; a *goal-setting* component, wherein the respondents identify the specific tasks to be performed; a *planning* component, whereby the respondents retrieve the relevant items from their language knowledge and plan their use; and an *execution* component, whereby the respondents implement the plan. Hence, this latest framework for strategic competence is broad and includes test-taking strategies within it.

CONTRIBUTIONS OF VERBAL REPORT
TO UNDERSTANDING TEST-TAKING STRATEGIES

Verbal reports have been used in an effort to better understand the processes involved in taking assessment instruments of different kinds. One purpose for obtaining such data is to provide guidelines on how to be more efficient and successful at test-taking. To a certain extent, various self-improvement courses on, say, the TOEFL test are based at least in part on empirically based insights as to what respondents do to produce answers and the results. A second, and perhaps the main purpose for using verbal reports in investigations of performance on assessment instruments, however, is to enable researchers to gain insights into improving the reliability and validity of such assessment instruments. Information gained from verbal reports is intended as feedback to those who construct and use assessment instruments concerning the strategies used to produce both correct and incorrect answers.

As researchers are only beginning to develop means for collecting more than just anecdotal data on test-taking strategies, we cannot say that verbal report methods have already yielded numerous valuable insights. We can, however, assert that these insights are beginning to appear in ever more systematic patterns, in both qualitative and more quantitative descriptions, and they have already led to the revision of items and procedures, as well as to the revision of instructions to respondents. This section gives examples of verbal reports as means of describing the strategies used in reading comprehension tasks, in reading–writing tasks such as summarization, and in oral production tasks.

STRATEGIES IN READING COMPREHENSION TASKS

Verbal report methods—primarily reflecting self-revelation and self-observation—have been employed as a means of describing strategies used in taking second language (L2) reading comprehension tests (Cohen, 1984). On open-ended reading comprehension tasks, for example, respondents have revealed through verbal reports that they may be prone to copy material directly from a text for use in a response. In a study of 19 college-level learners of Hebrew L2 that involved retrospective verbal reports 1 week after the learners took their final exam, it was found that students lifted material intact from an item stimulus or from a text passage for use in their written responses (Cohen & Aphek, 1979). Results might include verb forms incorrectly inflected for person, number, gender, or tense; verbs reflecting the correct root but an incorrect conjugation; and so forth. As a result, raters then may not know whether the respondent in fact understands the material and such copying may produce linguistically awkward responses.

In a research study, thirty 10th-grade EFL (English as a foreign language) students (15 high-proficiency readers and 15 low-proficiency readers) were asked to verbalize thoughts while finding answers to open-ended and multiple-choice questions (Gordon, 1987). The researcher found that answers to test questions did not necessarily reflect comprehension of the text. Both types of reading comprehension questions were regarded by the respondents as "mini" reading comprehension tests. With respect to test-taking strategies, the low-proficiency students tended to process information at the local (sentence/word) level, not relating isolated bits of information to the whole text. They used individual word-centered strategies like matching words in alternatives to text, copying words out of the text, translating word-for-word, or formulating global impressions of text content on the basis of key words or isolated lexical items in the text or in the test questions. The high-proficiency students, on the other hand, were seen to comprehend the text at a global level—predicting information accurately in context and using lexical and structural knowledge to cope with linguistic difficulties.

In an effort to provide immediate verbal report data, Nevo (1989) designed a testing format that would allow for immediate feedback after each item. She developed a response-strategy checklist, based on the test-taking strategies that have been described in the literature and on her intuitions as to strategies respondents were likely to select. A pilot study had shown that it was difficult to obtain useful feedback on an item-by-item basis without a checklist to jog the respondents' memory as to possible strategies.

Nevo's checklist included 15 strategies, each appearing with a brief description and a label meant to promote rapid processing of the checklist. As a research task, she administered a multiple-choice reading comprehension test in Hebrew first-language and French foreign-language to forty-two 10th graders, and requested that they indicate, for each of the 10 questions on each test, the strategy that was most instrumental in their arriving at an answer as well as that which was the second most instrumental. The responses were kept anonymous so as to encourage the students to report exactly what they did, rather than what they thought they were supposed to report.

It was found that students were able to record the two strategies that were most instrumental in obtaining each answer. The study indicated that respondents transferred test-taking strategies from their first language to the foreign language. The researcher also identified whether the selected strategies aided in choosing the correct answer. The selection of strategies that did not promote choice of the correct answer was more prevalent in the foreign-language test than in the first-language version. The main finding in this study was that it was possible to obtain feedback from respondents on their strategy use after each item on a test if a checklist was provided for quick labeling of the processing strategies utilized. Furthermore, the respondents reported benefitting greatly from the opportunity to become aware of how they took reading tests. They reported having been largely unaware of their strategies prior to this study.

Another study of test-taking strategies for reading comprehension tasks among non-natives revealed that respondents used certain strategies differently, depending on the type of question that was being asked. For example, the strategies of "trying to match the stem with the text" and "guessing" were reported more frequently for inference type questions than for the other question types such as direct statement or main idea. The strategy of "paraphrasing" was reported to occur more in responding to direct statement items than with inference and main idea question types (Anderson, Bachman, Perkins, & Cohen, 1991).

That study originated as a doctoral dissertation in which 28 native speakers of Spanish studying at an intensive ESL language school in Austin, TX, took as research tasks three measures of reading comprehension: a reading comprehension subtest from a test of language skills, a measure of ability to read college-level textbook prose (Textbook Reading Profile; Segal, 1986), and a second form of the standardized reading comprehension test (Anderson, 1989). After the first two tasks, the participants provided retrospective think-aloud protocols describing the strategies they used while reading the textbook material and answering the comprehension questions. The respondents also provided think-aloud protocols along with the final test. The data were categorized into a list of 47 processing strategies.

In the follow-up phase of the research, data from the participants' retrospective think-aloud protocols of their reading and test-taking strategies were combined with data from a content analysis and an item analysis to obtain a truly convergent measure of test validation (Anderson et al., 1991). The content analysis of the reading comprehension passages and questions was comprised of the test designer's analysis and one based on an outside taxonomy, and the item performance data included item difficulty and discrimination. This study marked perhaps the first time that both think-aloud protocols and more commonly used types of information on test content and test performance were combined in the same study in order to examine the validity of the test in a convergent manner.

STRATEGIES IN READING–WRITING TASKS AS IN SUMMARIZATION

In a study combining both strategies for reading and strategies for writing, verbal report methods were used to investigate how respondents at different levels of proficiency interacted with source tests in order to produce summary texts of their own, and how raters responded to these summaries (Cohen, 1994). The respondents were five native Portuguese-speaking students who had recently completed an English for Academic Purposes (EAP) course at a university in Brazil—a course emphasizing reading strategies and training in how to summarize. The two EAP course instructors who regularly rated the EAP exams of summarizing skill (both fluent speakers of Portuguese) participated in the study as raters. A sample test for assessing EFL proficiency was used as the testing instrument, consisting of three short texts and one longer one, three of which had to be summarized in Portuguese. The respondents were requested to provide verbal report data in their native language during the taking of the test. They also filled out a questionnaire indicating whether the EAP course had assisted them in writing the summaries, what they thought about taking tests of summarizing and about responding to the research assistant's queries regarding their test-taking strategies, and whether difficulties in performance on the summary tasks were due to reading problems or writing problems.

In addition, the raters were asked to provide verbal report data while assessing the tests. They were to indicate (a) the way that they determined what the various texts were about, (b) the steps that they were taking in their rating, and (c) their assessment of the respondents' understanding of these texts. The findings underscored the problem of reliability. A low-proficiency respondent was found to perform unexpectedly well. Second, there were marked differences between the two raters as to how they assessed this one respondent. Third, the raters differed somewhat in their basic criteria: Although they apparently agreed as to the material that should be included in the various summaries, one emphasized more than did the other the production of a summary that also constituted a coherent, readable text.

STRATEGIES IN ORAL PRODUCTION TASKS

With regard to oral language, the theoretical framework for *strategic competence* that was described earlier has been applied to the investigation of test-taking strategies on speaking tasks. According to the theoretical framework, when respondents are given a testing situation in which to perform an oral role play, they first assess the situation and identify the information that is needed in that context. They then do the following: (a) set their general goals, (b) plan out their specific response, (c) go about retrieving from their language knowledge the grammatical, discourse, and sociocultural features needed for the role play, and then (d) execute the role play. After they have finished, they may again perform an assessment to evaluate the extent to which the communicative goal was achieved.

As is the case with any theoretical model, test-takers may make differential use of the components of this model when performing specific testing tasks. The role of verbal reports would be to determine the strategies that respondents actually use in performing the task. For example, there are respondents who might not assess the situation before starting the role play. This strategy may work fine or, on the contrary, it may lead to the violation of certain sociocultural conventions. For instance, a respondent in a Japanese L2 role play may neglect to take into account the older age and higher status of the interlocutor, and may select language forms that are not adequately respectful. In addition, there are respondents who may set general goals for an utterance or string of utterances in an L2 role play without making a detailed plan of their utterances before producing them. Again, this strategy may work well or it may lead to ineffective utterances because they are lacking in, say, grammatical fine-tuning.

By the same token, role-play respondents may plan out the specifics of an interaction without having any general goals in mind. In such cases, the respondents may produce one or more L2 utterances that have been carefully monitored for grammatical accuracy but which do not fit into the overall discourse and, hence, come across as incoherent. There may be still other respondents who just start talking on an online basis, without determining either general goals or a detailed plan. Indeed, the same respondents may embrace one or another of these response patterns at different moments during a given test-taking situation and/or in different test-taking situations.

Research involving the use of verbal reports directly after the performance of oral role play interaction is just beginning to obtain empirical data regarding the extent of assessment and planning that actually takes place before, during, and after the execution of oral language tasks. Cohen and Olshtain (1993), for example, conducted a study on speech acts such as apologies, complaints, and requests, having respondents view a videotaped replay of their role playing in order to assist them in reconstructing the strategies that they used. The study was intended to describe ways in which nonnative speakers assess, plan, and execute such utterances. The subjects, 15 advanced English foreign-language learners, were given six speech act situations (two apologies, two complaints, and two requests) in which they were to role play along with a native speaker. (Note that this was just one form of oral production, namely, that of a role-play situation with one interlocutor, focused on a single situation.)

After each set of two interactions of the same type, the videotape was played back and then the respondents were asked both fixed and probing questions regarding the factors contributing to the production of their responses in those situations. The retrospective verbal report protocols were analyzed with regard to processing strategies in speech act formulation. The study found that with regard to the performance of speech act ability, respondents: (a) actually conducted only a general assessment of the utterances that were called for in half of the instances, and in the other half planned out specific vocabulary or grammatical structures, (b) often thought in two languages and sometimes in three languages (if trilingual) when planning and executing speech act utterances, (c) utilized a series of different strategies in searching for language forms, and (d) did not attend much to grammar or to pronunciation. Finally, there were respondents whose speech production styles might characterize them as *metacognizers* (individuals who seemed to have a highly developed metacognitive awareness and who used this awareness to the fullest), *avoiders* (those who avoided forms that they are not sure of), and *pragmatists* (those who got by in oral production more by means of online adjustment tricks than through metacognitive planning).

In another study investigating speaking performance (Cohen, 1998, chap. 5; Cohen, Weaver, & Li, 1996), 55 intermediate learners of foreign language at the University of Minnesota were either participants in a strategies-based instructional treatment or were Comparison students receiving the regular 10-week language course. The study used retrospective self-observation as a means for having respondents rate the frequency with which they used a series of before-, during-, and after-task strategies just after they completed each of three semidirect speaking tasks (self-description, story retelling, and city description) on a pre-posttest basis in a language laboratory situation. In this case, the oral production was not interactive at all, in contrast to the interactive speech act tasks in the above-mentioned Cohen and Olshtain (1993) study. Twenty-one of the Experimental and Comparison group students also provided verbal report data while they filled out the posttest Strategy Checklists, indicating their rationale for their responses to certain items, as well as their reactions to the instrument itself.

For the Experimental group, it was seen that an increase in certain preparatory strategies (e.g., translating specific words, writing out sentences, practicing the pronunciation of words, striving to select the right words and writing these words down) and monitoring strategies (e.g., monitoring for grammar, paying attention to the pronunciation of words, and analyzing a story for its key elements) related to an increase on one or more of the rating scales—self-confidence, grammar, vocabulary, and identifying and ordering elements in a story. For the Comparison group, an increase in the use of certain strategies during the self-description and city description tasks was positively related to an increase in ratings on task performance.

With regard to insights from the verbal report data collected along with the Strategy Checklist, it was the case that at least one Experimental subject conducted multiple practices before recording a particular response. In addition, the students reported avoiding new words they were not yet comfortable with, paraphrasing when they lacked a precise word, and sometimes avoiding pauses so as to sound more fluent. Students also reported having learned certain things about themselves as language learners, such as recognizing the benefits of relaxing more while performing language tasks.

With respect to the Comparison group, the use of translation into the native language mostly was considered a counterproductive activity, but one student reported using it as a way to get his mind thinking in the target language. Another student saw it as "cheating" to write out a response to an oral task ahead of time. Finally, there were students who voiced frustration at their limited language skills, something that did not come up in the Experimental group verbal report data. The verbal report data also provided some useful insights as to weaknesses in the Strategy Checklist itself, insights which could be put to good use in follow-up research.

Clearly, more work both along the lines of the Cohen and Olshtain (1993) and Cohen, Weaver, and Li (1996) studies and into more complex speaking situations, such as extended interviews or group interactions, is needed in order to learn more about the strategies that respondents use for the purpose of generating utterances in complex speech situations.

CONTINUING CRITICISM OF VERBAL REPORT MEASURES

Despite the extensive use of verbal report methods in what now amounts to a host of recent studies, consumers of research using verbal reports are still sometimes uncertain as to the inferences that they can legitimately make on the basis of these reports. While focusing on the use of verbal reports of first-language reading, Pressley and Afflerbach (1995) actually provide an excellent compendium of ideas for L2 researchers.[2] The authors refer to verbal reports as "a maturing methodology with much interesting work already accomplished and considerable work to be done" (p. 1). In their book, the authors demonstrate how the use of verbal report (whether as an exploratory methodology or as a means for testing hypotheses about reading) has yielded an elegant description of reading. They offer a detailed description of what they refer to as *before reading, during reading, after reading* monitoring and evaluating strategies, based on a review of 38 primary-data studies. As the authors put it, "The think-alouds were extremely revealing about the dynamics of comprehension difficulties and how understandings of text shift in reaction to comprehension difficulties and surprises in text" (p. 38).

At the same time that Pressley and Afflerbach (1995) refer to verbal report as a maturing method, they also rightly refer to it as an "underdeveloped" one (p. 119). For this reason, we now consider a series of problematic areas regarding the methodology, with an eye to where development needs to take place in order for the methodology to be more fully developed and hence to lend itself more readily to easier interpretation by the consumers of such research.

ISSUES IN VERBAL REPORT METHODOLOGY

A distinction has been made in the literature between self-revelational data in the form of immediate, online think-aloud protocols that involve no editing or analysis on the one hand and self-observational data in the form of introspective or retrospective self-observation on the other. Ericsson and Simon (1993) have advocated the collection of self-revelational data over other approaches to verbal report because asking questions only about what was heeded in short-term memory is seen as a means of making such reports more reliable in that there is no strain on the memory to reconstruct past thoughts.[3] In sharp contrast to this methodological position, the Pressley

---

[2]It should be noted that although this new book focuses on reading strategies in general, Afflerbach had previously written an article which included a focus on the use of verbal report in assessing reading comprehension (see Afflerbach & Johnston, 1984).

[3]The Ericsson and Simon book was originally written in 1984 and was reissued intact in 1993 with a 53-page preface, intended to update the book. The 1984 volume has served for many as authority on how verbal reports are supposed to be conducted. The Pressley and Afflerbach volume constitutes perhaps the first effort to determine the fit between Ericsson and Simon's methodological recommendations and actual uses made of the methodology in the field.

and Afflerbach (1995) survey of studies in first-language (L1) reading found considerable variation as to the immediacy of the reporting and the amount of interpretation respondents were asked to provide.

The researchers found not only self-revelational protocols but also self-observational reports which were collected after each sentence, after each episode, at signaled spots in the text (usually two or more sentences), after every 2 minutes, at the end of the text, or whenever the readers wanted. Thus, there was found to be fluctuation both within and across studies as to whether subjects were asked to provide think-aloud, introspective (i.e., within 20 seconds of the event), or retrospective reports (separated somewhat in time from the actual reading). Pressley and Afflerbach (1995) give one explanation for this departure from exclusive use of the think-aloud approach—namely, that in order to obtain verbal reports of otherwise automatized cognition, there is a need to slow down the process such as through the interruptive methods listed above.

Not only did Pressley and Afflerbach (1995) have difficulty in determining if verbal reports in the studies that they reviewed actually reflected traces remaining in short-term memory or rather reflected the subjects' reconstructions of what happened as they read; they were also unable to determine whether there was substantive difference in quality between think-aloud data produced when subjects performed no analysis and the self-observational data when they analyzed what they were thinking. The reasons they gave for their inability to make a comparison were: (a) there was too little systematic study of this issue in the given research reports, and (b) the verbal reporting itself was influenced differentially by the nature of the training, coaching, or prompting that the respondents received before and during the reporting phase.

A study on writing considered the issue of delay in the case of retrospective verbal reports after completing the writing task (Greene & Higgins, 1994). The investigators offered four suggestions for improving the reliability and validity of such data: (a) minimizing the time between the process and report by obtaining a report immediately after a writer completes a task, (b) designing prompts that can help writers better access detailed information from their short- and long-term memory (e.g., through the use of concrete examples and contextual cues), (c) making clear to the respondents the purpose of the retrospective accounts,[4] and (d) reporting one's findings in ways that enable readers to see how the conclusions have been derived from the data (e.g., by including enough data in a re-

---

[4]Current research policies at many institutions now require that respondents be fully informed as to what they will be asked to do and that they give their written consent. So in essence, the days of concealing the true motives from the respondents are waning. Furthermore, it may be counterproductive for the purposes of the study to have the subjects distracted for even a portion of the time by anxieties concerning the uses to be made of their responses.

port so that readers are able to make their own assessments about the value of research based on retrospection).

RESPONDENTS' ROLE IN INTERPRETING THE DATA

Some researchers are wary about having subjects interpret why they are doing something. Their rationale is that a request to provide interpretation is more likely to influence how the respondents perform continuing phases of the same task. In addition, they consider a "why" question as likely to produce unreliable answers if at the time the respondents are not thinking about why they are doing the action (Ericsson & Simon, 1993).[5] Thus, it is recommended by some that interpretation of verbal reports be left to researchers, rather than, say, having it be the respondents' responsibility to categorize their cognitions. Despite these recommendations, Pressley and Afflerbach's review of 38 primary data studies of L1 reading found that many studies went beyond having readers simply report their thoughts, and requested them to interpret their processes as well. Presumably, the insights from self-observation offer a rich enough source of information not available through think-aloud protocols alone that researchers are willing to risk threats to the reliability of the verbal report tasks in order to obtain the data.

Early descriptions of verbal report methods usually included the stipulation that respondents not be given instructions as to what to include in their verbal reports. They were to be left to their own devices since any instructions might lead to biased processing. However, anyone faced with analyzing transcriptions of undirected verbal report protocols has seen how such data are likely to be too general and incomplete. As a consequence, even methodological hard-liners like Ericsson and Simon (1993) are in favor of instructions directed to the respondents to make the verbal reports more complete.

Not so surprisingly, then, many studies now include instructions to elicit particular cognitive behaviors. For example, reading researchers have cued different processes in the different studies. Pressley and Afflerbach (1995) found one study which requested that subjects create a summary of what they read and were informed about the importance of summarization, a second which asked respondents to attend to content and style when reading, and others which required subjects to make inferences. The authors concluded that prompting respondents to use particular processes may be necessary: "...it is reasonable to prompt [processes] in order to assure that a sample of the target processes will, in fact, be observed" (p. 133).

---

[5]Actually both reliability and validity are of concern here. First, there is the concern that the measure produce data that are both consistent within any given verbal report session, as well as being consistent across sessions of a similar nature. The second concern is that the data be valid (i.e., that they actually constitute examples of what they purport to measure). Hence, reliability is a contributing factor in the determination of validity.

Ericsson and Simon (1993) have found that in order to ensure that the verbal report does not interfere with the task at hand, warm-up trials with tasks that yield easy-to-analyze think-aloud, introspective, and retrospective reports must follow the instructions. The researchers suggest that subjects be given trials on these warm-up tasks until they are able to make verbal reports without confounding them with explanations and justifications (Ericsson & Simon, 1993). This is to ensure consistency across subjects. "In some studies, more extensive warm-up procedures are used explicitly to *train* the subjects to conform to the think-aloud instructions" (p. 82). In a study in which subjects were asked not only to think aloud but also to try to give a reason for each response they made before entering it into the computer, the respondents who provided verbal reports after receiving training improved more on the computerized cognitive task than those who did not receive the training (Berry & Broadbent, 1984). In the review of 38 primary studies of verbal report in L1 reading, it was found that while in some studies the respondents were given an opportunity to practice, in others they were not (Pressley & Afflerbach, 1995).

THE EFFECTS OF VERBAL REPORT ON TASK PERFORMANCE

There are a series of issues relating to the effects of verbal report on task performance. We now look at four of them: (a) reactive effects, (b) positive effects, (c) the choice of language for verbal reporting, and (d) the authenticity of the assessment task, given the addition of the verbal reporting.

Reactive Effects of Verbal Reports: Verbal reports that involve intervening during the performance of a task have been criticized for the reactive effects that such intervention may cause. Stratman and Hamp-Lyons, for example, conducted an exploratory study to determine the extent of reactivity in writing. They had eight writers engage in two revision tasks 8 weeks apart, one with think-aloud verbal reports. All subjects were trained in how to provide think-aloud protocols. The researchers found for the subjects in their study that thinking aloud increased the number of new "word-level" errors (morphological, tense, and spelling; Stratman & Hamp-Lyons, 1994). Contrary to the investigators' expectations, thinking aloud was found to inhibit word or phrase additions in the revision process. They also found that although thinking aloud did not have an impact on complex meaning changes at the microstructural level, it stimulated the production of entirely new sentences (Stratman & Hamp-Lyons, 1994). They concluded that thinking aloud does alter the nature of processing in the revision phase of writing. They posited that think-aloud protocols may systematically influence the correction of organizational-level errors (i.e., the reordering of displaced sentences, the adjusting of faulty paragraph boundaries, the detection of faulty pronoun references, the detection of redundancies, the detection of word-level errors—in morphology, tense, and spelling—and the introduction of new word-level errors) and may also influence the amount and kind of microstructural meaning changes as well.

Positive Effects of Verbal Reports: Although the study by Stratman and Hamp-Lyons on the use of verbal reports during the revision phase of writing produced reactive results of a presumably negative nature, a series of other studies would suggest that there may be positive consequences of verbal reports. Collecting retrospections (termed *intervention protocols*) at various points during the writing has also been found to improve the reliability of the data collection task (Swanson-Owens & Newell, 1994). Swanson-Owens and Newell found that the interruption of writing for the purpose of reflecting on process served as a supportive measure in helping writers learn about composing, and thus to provide scaffolding for a subject's learning during data collection. Similarly positive outcomes of verbal reports have been reported for studies in the areas of vocabulary learning and reading as well. For example, Crutcher (1990) conducted a study of vocabulary learning with keywords and obtained retrospective reports for half of the items. He found that retention of the words was better for those items.

With regard to verbal reports in L2 reading, Nyhus (1994) looked at the attitudes of non-native readers of English toward the use of verbal reports to elicit their reading comprehension strategies. The respondents were seven third-quarter students in the Commanding English Program in General College at the University of Minnesota, a bridge program for refugee and immigrant non-native speakers of English. Five of the respondents were Vietnamese, one Chinese, and one Russian. Most had been in the United States for only 2 to 3 years. The study looked at their attitudes toward the effects of think-aloud and retrospective verbal report on their reading. They were also asked to assess verbal reports as a research methodology.

The respondents were shown a videotape of the researcher reading aloud and providing a think-aloud verbal report from a sociology text. Three excerpts from a sociology text were chosen for use with the respondents. Two were for practice readings and the third for the data collection. Red dots were placed between sentences to remind the respondents to verbalize their thoughts. Two sets of interview questions were developed, the first 12 questions to be asked following the respondents' initial think-aloud verbal report and the second 11 questions to be asked following the respondents' retrospective verbal report. The respondents were asked to read the text as they normally would but to say out loud, in English, all of their thoughts. They were told they could read the text silently, but all chose to read it out loud. The respondent and the researcher then listened to the recording of the verbal report, and the respondents provided a retrospective verbal report by pausing the tape when they wanted to make additional comments about thoughts which had occurred to them while reading the text. The researcher also had the respondents report on what they had been thinking but not verbalizing. Next, the researcher interviewed the respondents regarding their views about the think-aloud methodology. In addition, there was a second interview to elicit attitudes toward the retrospective methodology after the task had been completed.

For the most part, the respondents viewed the effects that they attributed to verbal report as beneficial. Most felt that think-aloud verbal reports affected their thinking about their reading in a positive way. It was reported to enhance their awareness and assessment of various aspects of the reading process, including an awareness of themselves as readers and of their interaction with the given text. Only two of the seven had negative comments about verbal reports, and these were the students whose English was the most limited. Since all verbal reports were conducted in English, performing the verbal report in English was most likely to the detriment of those with poorer English skills.

Despite several cases of difficulty in verbal reporting in English, all respondents viewed verbal reports as useful in various ways. They saw it as a means for placing students at a given level, as a diagnostic tool for determining their specific reading needs at a given level, and as a study technique to be used alone or in small groups. The students saw the group approach as a particularly beneficial method for discovering alternative ways of thinking about a text. Retrospective verbal reports, through having readers listen to and comment on a playback of their think-aloud verbal reports, provided still more insights. It was seen as a means of helping both readers, instructors, and researchers gain further insight into readers' thinking and reading processes.

Choice of Language for Reporting: An issue that the Nyhus study calls up is that there may, in fact, be a second-language threshold below which attempts to provide verbal reports in the target language will be counterproductive. Upton (1993), for example, found that when given a choice as to language for verbal reporting, the more advanced native-Japanese-speaking EFL subjects were likely to choose to provide verbal reports on English reading comprehension tasks in English, while the less proficient respondents preferred to use Japanese. Researchers may prefer at times to have the verbal reports in the target language, such as when the respondents are speakers of a variety of languages or when the language of the respondent group is not known to the researchers and obtaining translations is unfeasible. However, researchers need to be aware that practice of requiring verbal reports to be in the target language may be at the expense of collecting adequate data.

Authenticity of the Test-Taking Task: Beyond the other issues of reactivity, there is the one regarding the authenticity of the testing task when verbal reports are involved. Almost without question, the introduction of verbal reporting techniques alters the nature of the task so that it is no longer the task that it was, regardless of whether its inclusion has a beneficial or detrimental influence on the performance of the task. In fact, respondents may well be told that the task they are engaged in will not count for credit in order to ensure that their willingness to participate in the data collection process. The challenge for researchers, then, is to simulate task conditions as they would be if the instrument were administered without the addition of verbal reports and, furthermore, to request from respondents that they perform the tasks as much as possible in the way that they would if they were not providing verbal reports. For some assessment tasks, this is easier to do than with others.

For example, some forms of verbal reports are less intrusive than others. If respondents are simply to check off from an attached list those strategies that they used on a given item just after responding to the item, the activity may have a minimal influence on performance for that item. If, on the other hand, the respondent is to give an oral explanation of processing strategies whatever they may be and without the use of a checklist, then the verbal reporting may be more intrusive, possibly detracting from performance on the testing task itself.

TOWARD MORE ROBUST VERBAL REPORT METHODS AND MORE COMPLETE WRITE UPS

What seems to emerge from this discussion of methodological issues in verbal reports as applied to test-taking strategies is the need for both more refined measures and more details about the verbal report methods employed in each given study. Having this more detailed information furnished would facilitate comparisons of cross-study comparisons regarding both test-taking strategies and the research methodology itself. For example, Pressley and Afflerbach (1995) propose a study of reading strategies that would call for a carefully detailed comparison between think-aloud verbal reports and delayed reports. The study would assess the extent to which ongoing verbal reports might interfere with online reading and distort the natural reading processes, and the extent to which delayed stopping after every sentence or few sentences might shift the nature of subsequent reading, if at all. They would also wish to investigate the question as to how long reports can be delayed before they are altered by the delay. In making their plea for greater completeness in the description of verbal report methods, Pressley and Afflerbach include a listing of variables for which more complete and systematic information is desirable.

ISSUES OF METHOD AND OF WRITE UPS
FOR VERBAL REPORTS

Let us now relate Pressley and Afflerbach's listing of variables to studies of L2 assessment. The following list includes areas for refining verbal report methods and for enhancing write ups describing the methods in more detail adequate to ensure comparison across studies:

Subjects' Characteristics.   For the purpose of comparison across studies, the educational background of the respondents, their knowledge of the task at hand, and their motivation to do the task should be made clear. In addition, their level of language proficiency (especially in the case of L2 studies) and their age should be indicated. Pressley and Afflerbach (1995) also suggested that their short-term memory capacity and their spatial ability be noted, but this would entail special psychological testing which is usually not conducted in L2 assessment. In addition, Pressley and Afflerbach stressed the need for studies with larger numbers of subjects, since most studies are of individual cases or of small groups. Their point is that while the accumulation of small-scale studies using verbal reports does help to generate a large-scale picture, comparison across them can be somewhat problematic, especially if the approaches to data collection are different. The problem is that most researchers do not have the budget to conduct verbal report work with large groups.

Whereas Pressley and Afflerbach limit themselves to respondents who were performing a task in their native language and providing verbal reports in that language, research into L2 test-taking strategies is faced with the issue of choice of language for verbal reporting, as indicated above. When dealing with groups of speakers of numerous languages, the verbal report protocols may need to be in the target language. In cases where the respondents share the same native language or speak a limited number of languages, it may be advisable to give them a choice as to the language of the verbal report, since the less proficient they are in the target language, the more difficulty they may experience trying to do the task in the target language and provide verbal reports in the target language at the same time. As already noted, the study by Nyhus (1994) found that the two poorer ESL readers were the ones reporting difficulty providing the verbal reports, which was in the second language. Regardless of whether bilinguals use one language or the other for their verbal reports, it is important that the researcher indicate the extent to which one or the other is used.

Characteristics of the Materials.   When textual material serves as a stimulus for verbal report data, it would be helpful if the investigator specifies the genre of the material, its topic, its length, and its difficulty level for the given respondents. Although some or most of these variables may be provided as a matter of course (especially if texts are included in the appendix of the study), Pressley and Afflerbach would request that investigators indicate the fit between the task and the characteristics of the given respondents. Any such details could help other researchers to interpret the findings with greater ease, as well as to attempt replication of the study, if so desired. Perhaps more so in foreign than in native language reading, the genre of the text can make a big difference in the ease of reading. Even if the readers feel comfortable with the genre (e.g., journalistic writing), still they may have difficulty with the specific topic transmitted by means of that genre (e.g., an account of a holiday with which the reader is completely unfamiliar).

Criterion Task. It is imperative for the purpose of comparison that the researcher provide a clear indication of the tasks that the respondents were asked to perform (e.g., in reading research, whether it was free recall, recognition, question answering, summarization, or some combination of these), plus the directions given to the subjects. Pressley and Afflerbach found in the studies that they reviewed, that the instructions were either not provided or that reference to them was vague. The reason that the instructions are considered so crucial in verbal report work is expressly because of the orientation to the task that it is possible to give through the instructions. It is also important to have a clear description of any technical equipment employed in the study (e.g., a multimedia program on CD Rom). Likewise, the goals of the language task should be clear, as well as the modalities utilized. In addition, Smagorinsky (1998) stresses that because the cognition behaviors prompted by a given task are taking place in a specific sociocultural environment, it would be beneficial to provide details not only concerning the setting, the task, and the content reported, but also with regard to the relationship between the participants, the participants' conception of the researcher, the trust accorded to the listener, the rules for what it was appropriate to say, and the emotion involved in the report.

Guidance in Verbal Reporting. It is valuable both for purpose of comparison across studies and for replication that information be given as to the nature and extent of guidance that the subjects received in verbal reporting. It is useful to know, for example, whether the subjects received feedback in practice sessions, whether they were coached during the data collection sessions, and if so, the length of the guidance (e.g., until they got the behavior correct or until they acted as they were supposed to act). It has become more common to instruct respondents in how to provide verbal reports as well as to coach them as they are providing it (e.g., requesting that they not report on the basis of what they usually do, but rather that they stick to what they are actually doing at the given instance).

Methods of Analysis. In order for other researchers to interpret the findings, it may prove beneficial to include details as to the development of the categories and coding schemes used in interpreting verbal reports. It may also be beneficial to include the codes and symbols used in the transcriptions of the verbal report protocols (e.g., symbols for suprasegmental features, such as tone of voice). Of course, verbal report data may also be collected in the written modality, as has been done in various studies (e.g., Robinson, 1991). In such cases, there would be no suprasegmentals. In any event, Pressley and Afflerbach found that there was usually incomplete reporting of any scoring codes that may have been developed for the purpose of analyzing the data.

Categories Used to Score Verbal Report Protocols. It is helpful for researchers to indicate how the actual scoring of verbal report protocols is done, because there is so much interpretive work involved. If the respondents themselves listen to their verbal reports in order to assist in the interpretation of protocols, as Nyhus (1994) did in her study on the effects of verbal reports on L2 reading, it would be important to highlight this feature and to describe it fully in the write up phase. Such a procedure has the value of improving the validity of the measure, because the respondents themselves are verifying the accuracy of what they reported (choice of words, completeness of the report, and the like) and possibly adding what they had neglected to mention the first time around. It might even pay to have researchers provide verbal reports while they are engaged in the task of making their decisions about how to score given instances of behavior appearing in the protocols. Verbal report protocols of raters of second language, for instance, reveal instances where the raters do not understand the categories that they are supposed to be using in their ratings (e.g., "style" or "register").

Inter-Rater Reliability Checks. In cases where two or more investigators score the data, it would be advisable to run inter-rater reliability checks to determine the extent to which the investigators are using similar criteria in arriving at scores. Information about such inter-rater reliability checks should be provided in the research report.

Selection of Verbal Report Excerpts for Inclusion in Research Reports. A somewhat subtle issue is that of how the data are chosen for inclusion in reports. Other researchers would want to know how representative such excerpts are of the data set as a whole. There is a concern that the investigators may slant the findings according to the excerpts from the data that they choose to select for inclusion in any reports that they write. It is for this reason that Greene and Higgins (1994) went to some lengths to demonstrate how to represent verbal report data in an equitable way in their study of retrospective verbal reports of L1 writing processes.

Theories Used in Framing Verbal Report Studies. The researchers are asked to identify the theoretical principles that the verbal report techniques were intended to investigate. In order to help validate the verbal report measures utilized in the study, Pressley and Afflerbach consider it the researchers' responsibility to provide information as to whether the verbal report measures really reflect the cognitive processes that are being reported. They contend that the researchers should indicate the relationship between the verbal report and the performance outcomes, much as they do in their own book by demonstrating that theoretical models of reading (e.g., Anderson & Pearson, Baker & Brown, van Dijk & Kintsch, and their own model of constructively responsive reading) were supported by verbal report data obtained from reading studies. As Pressley and Afflerbach (1995) put it, "As validation efforts proceed, we urge careful attention to the establishment of clear linkages between theory, verbal process reports, and other measures that can be complementary to verbal self-reports. We believe this work will do much to bring verbal reports from the status of a 'bootstrap operation' (Ericsson & Simon, 1993) to a maturing methodology" (p. 126).

Most published studies of second language acquisition include a statement of the research questions with the rationale for each. If the verbal report measures are simply aimed at exploring some aspect of these research questions, then the theoretical underpinnings are probably provided. It is possible, however, that the theoretical rationale for a given verbal report procedure is not overtly clear to the reader of the report. In such cases, the request would be to provide this rationale.

THE VALIDITY OF VERBAL REPORTS

Although the discussion of nine issues focused mostly on the reliability of the verbal report measures, their validity also comes into play in each and every issue. Larger samples help to make the results more valid; however, a trade-off to increasing the sample size would be to amass a series of well planned and executed small-scale studies. As for the role played by the materials and the tasks in the determination of validity, it is imperative that the consumers of the research results have adequate information about the nature of the materials and about the specific instructions that the respondents were given for performing the task. Such information is crucial in interpreting the verbal report responses received. By the same token, the consumers of the reports need to know the extent to which the respondents were coached in how to perform the task.

Once the data are collected, the analysis procedures also have a direct impact on whether the data measure what they purport to measure—that is to say, the rationale for the construction of the analysis categories and then the actual process of data analysis. Did the raters understand and properly use all of the rating categories? With regard to inter-rater reliability, if there is more than one rater, a low inter-rater reliability coefficient would call into question not only the reliability of the ratings but their validity as well.

Furthermore, there is the issue of whether the reported data are comprehensive or selective, and if selective, what this says about the validity of the reporting process. Finally, there is concern that the study not simply use verbal reports for their own sake but rather because the data collection method does, in fact, help to gather data bearing on the theoretical issue at hand.

IMPLICATIONS FOR RESEARCHERS

The chapter started by contrasting the three forms of verbal report—self-report, self-observation, and self-revelation—and by defining test-taking strategies. It then considered the contribution that verbal report methods have made to the understanding of test-taking strategies. The chapter then focused on concerns about the appropriate use of such measures and about the nature of reports which include the findings from the use of such measures. The issues included the immediacy of the verbal reporting, the respondents' role in interpreting the data, prompting for specifics in verbal report, guidance in verbal reporting, and the reactive effects of verbal reporting.

The lengthy focus on both refining verbal report methods and on improving the write up of verbal report procedures was intended to underscore the importance of being rigorous both in design and in description. The purpose would be not only to improve the data, but also to assist other researchers in (a) understanding fully what was done, (b) being able to make comparisons to other studies, and (c) being able to replicate the studies. In addition, the point was made that care in the write up can help to dispel arguments that such methodological approaches are not adequately rigorous.

Whereas the research literature on verbal protocols has tended to focus on justifying verbal reports in the face of criticism from those opposed to it, this chapter has instead focused on the fine-tuning of verbal report methods. By now so many studies using verbal report techniques have emerged that the time has come to provide greater systematicity both in the collection of such data and in the reporting of such studies through the research literature. This chapter has intended to help researchers ask and get answers to the more finely tuned questions so that the already valuable findings from verbal report studies on test-taking strategies—and other areas of second language investigation as well—will be even more greatly enhanced by the extra methodological rigor.

IMPLICATIONS FOR CLASSROOM TEACHERS

What can teachers take from this chapter and put into practice? Since the classroom can be an excellent place to get feedback as to how a test has actually worked, it would be possible to use practice tests to do just that. For example, a practical task would be to split a language class into pairs, with one of the two being the respondent and the other the investigator. The exercise would be aimed at identifying the strategies that respondents used to produce answers and what this says about what they know of the language and the way they behave as learners.

Let us say that the assessment task is one of reading a short text and then answering several reading comprehension questions (whether multiple-choice, short answer, or essay). The task would direct the respondents to think aloud as they read (i.e., sharing with their partner in the investigator role whatever thoughts come up as they read). It may be necessary to have a short training session at the outset to determine if the respondents understand what it means for them to think aloud, or in retrospect as to their strategies for answering the test items. One kind of practice exercise for verbal reporting would have the readers describe one of three tasks and have the investigators close their eyes and imagine what it is that the respondents are describing. The tasks could, for example, include "tying your shoelaces," "combing/brushing your hair," or "determining how much change you have in your wallet/purse (i.e., how many coins and what denominations)". The investigators, with their eyes closed, are to make sure that the respondents verbalize their actions aloud and that every step is included. The investigators are to coach the respondents if the process is not being described clearly enough.

The nature of the verbal reports on the test analysis task will vary according to the respondents. With regard to the reading of the text, some respondents will mumble the words of the text and voice aloud the thoughts that they have while they are reading. For others, it means reading silently and then providing an oral recap each time there is a natural pause in the reading process. Then while they are answering the questions, some respondents will provide think-aloud responses as to what their understanding of the questions is and as to any strategies they devise for dealing with the questions at every step of the way. Others may wait and provide a recap of what they did to produce the answer after they have done it.

With regard to the recap on how they did the task, the following are some areas that could be probed. For example, did the respondents read the text through thoroughly at the outset or did they go right to the questions? In reading the text, did they use any support strategies such as underlining words, and if so, which ones? Did they read through the text in linear fashion or jump around? Did they use strategies for simplifying the text through paraphrase? Did they attempt to establish coherence in the text, such as through content schemata (knowledge of the topic) or textual clues (organization, context, discourse functions)? Were they aware of supervising their use of reading strategies (i.e., planning the strategies, monitoring their use, and evaluating the results of their reading, the so-called "metacognitive" strategies)? Did they vary the type of reading that they used? For instance, did they skim certain portions and read others in depth?

After a description of this kind has been obtained through the interaction of the respondent and the investigator, the next step is to see how accurately the respondent answered each question and to link their performance to their selection and application of strategies to the task. Either the teacher can provide the "correct" response or an acceptable set of responses for the item, or the students in the class themselves could provide this. Did the respondents miss any answers or come up with other answers that they felt were acceptable? Taking into consideration how the respondents came up with the answers that they arrived at, was there a link between the way that they read and the results? Did they gain any insights about how they read in such assessment tasks?

This practical exercise is not intended for the purpose of collecting research data but rather as a means of obtaining rich data as to how a given test actually functions—what the students actually do to produce answers to it. Teachers can use verbal reports here to provide an important source of information in this process of examining the exam or testing the test.

Chapter 8

Epilogue:
Promoting Learner-Directed Assessment

Glayol Ekbatani
St. John's University

Herbert Pierson
St. John's University

In summing up, we would like to recapitulate the modest, but important, goals of this volume. They have been four-fold:

1. To promote the pedagogical value of learner-directed assessment as an approach that links instruction to evaluation.

2. To share the concerns raised by experts in the field as to the validity and limitations of existing norm-referenced assessment procedures, thereby adding to the validity of assessment instruments.

3. To encourage a departure from traditional testing formats and movement towards alternative forms of assessment.

4. To provide practitioners, whether they be program directors or busy classroom teachers, with the possible means of alternative assessment.

We hope that readers will take advantage of both the practical and re-search-oriented assessment tools presented in this book and use them in both the classroom and for general evaluation. These tools are: (a) the descriptors and proficiency scales configured by Brian North; (b) the self-assessment questionnaire designed by Diane Strong-Krause; (c) the portfolio routines and procedures formulated by Margo Gottlieb, Alan Hirvela, and Herbert Pierson; (d) the evaluation of complex speech act through videotaped role play devised by Andrew Cohen; and, (e) the insights on spontaneous self-repair reported by Erna Van Hest.

One measure of the success of this volume is whether it is able to motivate those involved in ESL education with the determination to seriously look at the potential of self-directed assessment as both a valid and reliable addition and supplement to traditional assessment. At this point, learner-directed education will not replace traditional assessment, but learner-directed assessment nevertheless is valuable input that can be integrated into the overall assessment profile of individual ESL learners. However, if a significant number of ESL professionals adopted some aspects of learner-directed assessment, they would approach a more accurate picture of what individual language learners can do. Herein lies the present and future value of learner-directed assessment.

References

Afflerbach, P., & Johnston, P. (1984). On the use of verbal reports in reading research. *Journal of Reading Behavior, 16*(4), 307–322.

Alderson, J. C. (1991). Bands and scores. In J. C. Alderson & B. North (Eds.), *Language testing in the 1990s* (pp. 71–86). London: Modern English Publications/British Council, Macmillan.

Alderson, J. C., & North, B. (1991). (Eds.), *Language testing in the 1990s.* London: Modern English Publications/British Council, Macmillan.

Allan, A. (1992). Development and validation of a scale to measure test-wiseness in EFL/ESL reading test takers. *Language Testing, 9*(2), 101–122.

Anderson, N. J. (1989*). Reading comprehension tests versus academic reading: What are second language readers doing?* Unpublished doctoral dissertation, University of Texas, Austin.

Anderson, N. J., Bachman, L., Perkins, K., & Cohen, A. D. (1991). An exploratory study into the construct validity of a reading comprehension test: Triangulation of data sources. *Language Testing, 8*(1), 41–66.

Arter, J. A., & Spandel, V. (1992). Using portfolios of student work in instruction and assessment. *Educational Measurement: Issues and Practice, Spring,* 36–44.

Bachman, L. F. (1990). *Fundamental considerations in language testing.* Oxford: Oxford University Press.

Bachman, L., & Palmer, A. (1989). The construct validation of self-ratings of communicative language ability. *Language Testing, 6* (1), 14–29.

Bachman, L. F., & Palmer, A. S. (1996). *Language testing in practice.* Oxford: Oxford University Press.

Bachman, L., & Savignon S. J. (1986). The evaluation of communicative language proficiency: A critique of the ACTFL oral interview. *Modern Language Journal, 70,* 380–390.

Batzle, J. (1992). *Portfolio assessment and evaluation: Developing and using portfolios in the classroom.* Cypress, CA: Creative Teaching.

Beall, J. (1994). Portfolios, research, and writing about science. In L. Black, D. A. Daiker, J. Sommers, & G. Stygall (Eds.), *New directions in portfolio assessment* (pp. 93–102). Portsmouth, NH: Boynton/Cook.

Belanoff, P. (1994). Portfolios and literacy: Why? In L. Black, D. A. Daiker, J. Sommers, & G. Stygall (Eds.), *New directions in portfolio assessment* (pp. 13–24). Portsmouth, NH: Boynton/Cook.

Belanoff, P., & Dickson, M. (Eds.). (1991). *Portfolios: Process and product.* Portsmouth, NH: Heinemann.

Berry, D. C., & Broadbent, D. E. (1984). On the relationship between task performance and associated verbalizable knowledge. *Quarterly Journal of Experimental Psychology, 36*, 209–231.

Black, L., Daiker, D. A., Sommers, J., & Stygall, G. (Eds.). (1994). *New directions in portfolio assessment.* Portsmouth, NH: Boynton/Cook.

Blanche, P., & Merino, B. J. (1989). Self-assessment of foreign language skills: Implications for teachers and researchers. *Language Learning, 39*, 313–340.

Bond, L. A., Braskamp, D., van der Ploeg, A., & Roeber, E. (1995). *State student assessment programs database school year 1994-1995.* Oakbrook, IL: North Central Regional Educational Laboratory.

Borman, W. C. (1979). Format and training effects on rating accuracy and rater errors. *Journal of Applied Psychology, 64*, 410–421.

Borman, W. C. (1986). Behavior-based rating scales. In R. Berk (Ed.), *Performance assessment: Methods and applications.* Baltimore: The Johns Hopkins University Press.

Brindley, G. (1986). *The assessment of second language proficiency: Issues and approaches.* Adelaide, Australia: National Curriculum Resource Centre.

Brindley, G. (1989). *Assessing achievement in the learner centred curriculum.* NCELTR, Macquarie University: Sydney.

Brindley, G. (1991). Defining language ability: The criteria for criteria. In S. Anivan (Ed.), *Current developments in language testing.* Singapore: Regional Language Centre.

Burnham, C. (1986). Portfolio evaluation: Room to breathe and grow. In C. Bridges (Ed.), *Training the new teacher of college composition* (pp. 71–82). Urbana, IL: National Council of Teachers of English.

Callahan, S. (1997). Tests worth taking? Using portfolios for accountability in Kentucky. *Research in the Teaching of English, 31*, 295–336.

Camp, R., & Levine, D. S. (1991). Portfolios evolving. In P. Belanoff & M. Dickson (Eds.), *Portfolios: Process and product* (pp. 194–205). Portsmouth, NH: Boynton/Cook.

Canale, M. & Swain, M. (1980). Theoretical bases of communicative approaches to second language teaching and testing. *Applied Linguistics, 1*, 1–47.

Cason, G. J., & Cason, C. J. (1984). A deterministic theory of clinical performance rating. *Evaluation and the Health Professions, 7*, 221–247.

Champney, H. (1941). The measurement of parent behavior. *Child Development, 12*, 131–166.

Chiseri-Strater, E. (1992). College sophomores reopen the closed portfolio. In D. H. Graves & B.S. Sunstein (Eds.), *Portfolio portraits* (pp. 61–72). Portsmouth, NH: Heinemann.

Clark, E., & Andersen, E. (1979, Spring). *Spontaneous repairs:Awareness in the process of acquiring language.* Paper presented at the Biennial Meeting of the Society for Research in Child Development, San Francisco.

Clark, J. D., & O'Mara, F. (1991). Measurements and research, implications of Spolsky's conditions for second language learning. *Applied Language Learning, 2*, 71–113.

Clemmons, J., Laase, L., Cooper, D., Areglado, N., & Dill, M. (1993). *Portfolios in the classroom: A teacher's sourcebook.* New York: Scholastic.

Cohen, A. D. (1984). On taking language tests: What the students report. *Language Testing, 1*(1), 70–81.

Cohen, A. D. (1987). Studying language learning strategies: How do we get the information? In A. L. Wenden & J. Rubin (Eds.), *Learner strategies in language learning* (pp. 31–40). Englewood Cliffs, NJ: Prentice-Hall International.

Cohen, A. D. (1994). English for academic purposes in Brazil: The use of summary tasks. In C. Hill & K. Parry (Eds.), *From testing to assessment: English as an international language* (pp. 174–204). London: Longman.

Cohen, A. D. (1998). *Strategies in learning and using a second language.* Harlow, England: Longman.

Cohen, A. D., & Aphek, E. (1979). *Easifying second language learning.* [Research report under the auspices of Brandeis University and submitted to the Jacob Hiatt Institute, Jerusalem]. (ERIC Document Reproduction Service No. ED 163 753).

Cohen, A. D., & Holstein, E. (1993). The production of speech acts by EFL learners. *TESOL Quarterly, 27*(1), 33–56.

Cohen, A. D., & Hosenfeld, C. (1981). Some uses of mentalistic data in second-language research. *Language Learning, 31*(2), 285–313.

Cohen, A. D., Weaver, S. J., & Li, T-Y. (1996). *The impact of strategies-based instruction on speaking a foreign language.* Minneapolis: Center for Advanced Research on Language Acquisition, University of Minnesota (CARLA Working Paper Series #4). (Also, in revised form in A. D. Cohen, 1998, *Strategies in learning and using a second language).* Harlow: Longman.

Condon, W., & Hamp-Lyons, L. (1991). Introducing a portfolio-based writing assessment: Progress through problems. In P. Belanoff & M. Dickson (Eds.), *Portfolios: Process and product* (pp. 231–247). Portsmouth, NH: Boynton/Cook.

Condon, W., & Hamp-Lyons, L. (1994). Maintaining a portfolio-based writing assessment: Research that informs program development. In L. Black, D. A. Daiker, J. Sommers, J., & G. Stygall (Eds.), *New directions in portfolio assessment* (pp. 277–285). Portsmouth, NH: Boynton/Cook.

Conway, G. (1994). Portfolio cover letters, students' self-presentation, and teachers' ethics. In L. Black, D. A. Daiker, J. Sommers, & G. Stygall (Eds.), *New directions in portfolio assessment.* Portsmouth, NH: Boynton/Cook.

Coombe, C.A. (1992). The relationship between self-assessment ratings of functional literacy skills and basic English skills test results in adult refugee ESL learners (Doctoral dissertation, Ohio State University, 1992). *Dissertation Abstracts International, 53,* 3774A.

Council of Europe. (1992). *Transparency and coherence in language learning in Europe: Objectives, assessment and certification.* Strasbourg: Author.

Council of Europe. (1996). *A common European framework for language learning and teaching: Draft of a framework proposal.* Strasbourg.: Author.

Crutcher, R. J. (1990). *The role of mediation in knowledge acquisition and retention: Learning foreign vocabulary using the keyword method* (Tech. Rept. No. 90–10.). Boulder: University of Colorado, Institute of Cognitive Science.

Cumming, A. (1995). Fostering writing expertise in ESL composition instruction: Modeling and evaluation. In D. Belcher & G. Braine (Eds.), *Academic writing in a second language* (pp. 375–397). Norwood, NJ: Ablex

Cummins, J. (1989). *Empowering minority students.* Sacramento: California Association for Bilingual Education.

Dailey, S. R. (1997). Portfolios in law school: Creating a community of writers. In K. B. Yancey (Ed.), *Situating portfolios* (pp. 214–222). Logan: Utah State University Press.

D'Aoust, C. (1992). Portfolios: Process for students and teachers. In K. B. Yancey (Ed.), *Portfolios in the writing classroom* (pp. 39–48). Urbana, IL: National Council of Teachers of English..

De Fina, A. A. (1992). *Portfolio assessment: Getting started.* New York: Scholastic.

Dellinger, D. (1993). Portfolios: A personal history. In M. A. Smith & M. Ylvisaker (Eds.), *Teachers' voices: Portfolios in the classroom* (pp. 11–24). Berkeley, CA: National Writing Project.

Dickinson, L. (1987). *Self-instruction in language learning.* London: Cambridge University Press.

Dickinson, L. (1992). *Learner autonomy.* Dublin: Authentik.

Dorroh, J. (1993). Portfolios in biology. In M.A. Smith & M. Ylvisaker (Eds.), *Teachers' voices: Portfolios in the classroom* (pp. 81–91). Berkeley, CA: National Writing Project.

Ekbatani, G., & Pierson, H. (1998). Teacher portfolios—vehicles of faculty assessment, reflection and growth. (ERIC Document Reproduction Service No. ED 163 753).

Elbow, P. (1994). Will the virtues of portfolios blind us to their potential dangers? In L. Black, D. A. Daiker, J. Sommers, & G. Stygall (Eds.), *New directions in portfolio assessment* (pp. 40–55). Portsmouth, NH: Boynton/Cook.

Elbow, P., & Belanoff, P. (1997). Reflections on the explosion: Portfolios in the '90s and beyond. In K. B. Yancey (Ed.), *Situating portfolios* (pp. 21–33). Logan: Utah State University Press.

Ericsson, K. A., & Simon, H. A. (1993). *Protocol analysis: Verbal reports as data.* Cambridge, MA: MIT Press.

Eurocentres. (1997). *Itembanker (Version 2.0): A testing tool for language teachers.* Zürich: Eurocentres Learning Service.

Evans, M. (1985). Self-initiated speech repairs: A reflection of communicative monitoring in young children. *Developmental Psychology, 21,* 365–371.

Farr, R., & Tone, B. (1994). *Portfolio performance assessment: Helping students evaluate their progress as readers and writers.* Fort Worth: Harcourt Brace.

Flower, L., & Hayes, J. R. (1984). Images, plans, and prose: The representation of meaning in writing. *Written Communication, 1*(1), 120–160.

Frank, M. (1994). *Using writing portfolios to enhance instruction and assessment.* Nashville, TN: Incentive.

Freedman, S. W. (1993). Linking large-scale testing and classroom portfolio assessments of student writing. *Educational Assessment, 1*(1), 27–52.

Freeman, Y. S., & Freeman, D. E. (1992). Portfolio assessment for bilingual learners. *Bilingual Basics, 8.*

French, R. L. (1992). Portfolio assessment and LEP students. *Proceedings of the Second National Research Symposium on Limited English Proficient Student Issues: Focus on Evaluation and Measurement* (pp. 249–272). Washington, DC: United States Department of Education.

Fu, D. (1992). One bilingual child talks about his portfolio. In D. H. Graves & B. S. Sunstein (Eds.), *Portfolio portraits* (pp. 171–183). Portsmouth, NH: Heinemann.

Fulcher, G. (1987). Tests of oral performance: The need for data-based criteria. *ELT Journal, 41,* 287–291.

Fulcher, G. (1993). *The construction and validation of ratings for oral tests in English as a foreign language*. Unpublished doctoral dissertation, University of Lancaster.

Garner, R. (1982). Verbal-report data on reading strategies. *Journal of Reading Behavior, 14*(2), 159–167.

Gay, P. (1991). A portfolio approach to teaching a biology-linked basic writing course. In P. Belanoff & M. Dickson (Eds.), *Portfolios: Process and product* (pp. 182–193).

Genesee, F., & Upshur, J. A. (1996). *Classroom-based evaluation in second language education*. New York: Cambridge University Press.

Gill, K. (Ed.). (1993). *Process and portfolios in writing instruction*. Urbana, IL: NCTE.

Glazer, S. M., & Brown, C. S. (1993). *Portfolios and beyond: Collaborative assessment in reading and writing*. Norwood, MA: Christopher-Gordon.

Goodman, Y. (1995). Foreword. In C. Porter & J. Cleland, *The portfolio as a learning strategy* (pp. ix–xi). Portsmouth, NH: Boynton/Cook.

Gordon, C. (1987). *The effect of testing method on achievement in reading comprehension tests in English as a foreign language*. Unpublished master's thesis, Tel-Aviv University, Ramat-Aviv, Israel.

Gottlieb, M. (1995). Nurturing student learning through portfolios. *TESOL Journal, 5*, 12–14.

Graves, D. H. (1992). Portfolios: Keep a good idea growing. In D. H. Graves & B. S. Sunstein (Eds.), *Portfolio portraits* (pp. 1-12). Portsmouth, NH: Heinemann.

Graves, D. H., & Sunstein, B. S. (Eds.). (1992). *Portfolio portraits*. Portsmouth, NH: Heinemann.

Greene, S., & Higgins, L. (1994). "Once upon a time": The use of retrospective accounts in building theory in composition. In P. Smagorinsky (Ed.), *Speaking about writing: Reflections on research methodology* (pp. 115–140). Thousand Oaks, CA: Sage.

Griffin, P. E. (1989, July). *Monitoring proficiency development in language*. Paper presented at the Annual Congress of the Modern Language Teachers Association of Victoria, Monash University. Victorica, New South Wales.

Griffin, P. E. (1990). Profiling literacy development: Monitoring the accumulation of reading skills. *Australian Journal of Education; 34*, 290–311.

Guskey, T. R. (Ed.). (1994). *High stakes performance assessment: Perspectives on Kentucky's educational reform*. Thousand Oaks, CA: Corwin.

Hain, B. (1991). Portfolios and the M.A. in English. In P. Belanoff & M. Dickson (Eds.), *Portfolios: Process and product* (pp. 93–98). Portsmouth, NH: Boynton/Cook.

Hamp-Lyons, L. (1991). Scoring procedures for ESL contexts. In L. Hamp-Lyons (Ed.), *Assessing second language writing in academic contexts* (pp. 241–276). Norwood, NJ: Ablex.

Hamp-Lyons, L. (1994). Interweaving assessment and instruction in college ESL writing classes. *College ESL, 4*, 43–55.

Hamp-Lyons, L., & Kroll, B. (1996). Issues in ESL writing assessment: An overview. *College ESL, 6*, 52–72.

Heiges, J. M. (1997). Portfolio for doctoral candidacy: A veritable alternative. In K. B. Yancey (Ed.), *Situating portfolios* (pp. 125–141). Logan: Utah State University Press.

Heilenman, L. K. (1990). Self-assessment of second language ability: The role of response effects. *Language Testing, 7*, 174–201.

Henning, G. (1990). Priority issues in the assessment of communicative language abilities. *Foreign Language Annals 23*, 379–384.

Henning, G. (1992). Dimensionality and construct validity of language tests. *Language Testing, 9*, 1–11.

Herman, J. L., & Winters, L. (1994). Portfolio research: A slim collection. *Educational Leadership, 52*, 48–55.

Heron, J. (1981) Assessment revisited. In D. Boud (Ed.), *Developing student autonomy in learning.* New York: Nichols Publishing.

Hieke, A. (1981). A context-processing view of hesitation phenomena. *Language and Speech, 24*, 147–160.

Hirvela, A. (1997). "Disciplinary portfolios" and EAP writing instruction. *English for Specific Purposes, 16*, 83–100.

Huot, B. (1994a). An introduction to "Assessing Writing." *Assessing Writing, 1*, 1–9.

Huot, B. (1994b). Beyond the classroom: Using portfolios to assess writing. In L. Black, D. A. Daiker, J. Sommers, & G. Stygall (Eds.), *New directions in portfolio assessment* (pp. 325-333). Portsmouth, NH: Boynton/Cook.

Huot, B., & Williamson, M. M. (1997). Rethinking portfolios for evaluating writing: Issues of assessment and power. In K. B. Yancey (Ed.), *Situating portfolios* (pp. 43–56). Logan: Utah State University Press.

Ingalls, B. (1993). Interviewing a portfolio. In K. Gill (Ed.), *Process and portfolios in writing instruction* (pp. 63–68). Urbana, IL: National Council of Teachers of English.

Jaeger, R. M. (1989). Certification of student competence. In R. L. Linn (Ed). *Educational measurement* (3rd ed.). New York: Macmillan.

Janssen-van Dieten, A. (1989). The development of a test of Dutch as a second language: The validity of self-assessments by inexperienced subjects. *Language Testing, 6*, 30–46.

Johns, A. M. (1995a). An excellent match: Literacy portfolios and ESP. *English Teaching Forum, 33*, 16–21.

Johns, A. M. (1995b). Teaching classroom and authentic genres: Initiating students into academic cultures and discourses. In D. Belcher & G. Braine (Eds.), *Academic writing in a second language* (pp. 277–291). Norwood, NJ: Ablex.

Johns, A. M. (1997). *Text, role, and context.* Cambridge, England: Cambridge University Press.

Jones, N. (1993). *An item bank for testing English language proficiency: Using the Rasch model to construct an objective measure.* Doctoral dissertation, University of Edinburgh.

Kenyon, D. M., & Stanfield, C. W. (1992). *Examining the validity of a scale used in a performance assessment from many angles using the many-faceted Rasch model.* Washington, DC: Center for Applied Linguistics.

Krausert, S. (1992). Determining the usefulness of self-assessment of foreign language skills: Post-secondary ESL students placement contribution. *Dissertation Abstracts International, 52*, 3143A.

Lambert, R. (1993). Foreign language competency. In S. J. Moore & C. A. Morfit, *Language and international studies: A Richard Lambert Perspective* (pp. 150–161). Washington, DC: National Foreign Language Center Monograph Series.

Landy, F. J., & Farr, J. (1983). *The measurement of work performance.* San Diego: Academic Press.

Lantolf, J., & Frawley, W. (1985). Oral proficiency testing: A critical analysis. *Modern Language Journal, 70,* 337–345.

Lantolf, J., & Frawley, W. (1988): Proficiency, understanding the construct. *Studies in Second Language Acquisition, 10,* 181–196.

Larson, R. L. (1991). Using portfolios in the assessment of writing in the academic disciplines. In P. Belanoff & M. Dickson (Eds.), *Portfolios: Process and product* (pp. 137–149). Portsmouth, NH: Boynton/Cook.

LeBlanc, R., & Painchaud, G. (1985). Self-assessment as a second language placement instrument. *TESOL Quarterly, 19,* 73–87.

Levelt, W., & Cutler, A. (1983). Prosodic marking in speech repair. Journal of Semantics, *2,* 205–217.

Linacre, J .J. (1989). *Multi-faceted measurement.* Chicago: MESA Press.

Lucas, C. (1992). Introduction: Writing portfolios—Changes and challenges. In K. B. Yancey (Ed.), *Portfolios in the writing classroom* (pp. 1–11). Urbana, IL: National Council of Teachers of English.

Lyons, W. (1986). *The disappearance of introspection.* Cambridge, MA: MIT Press.

McClelland, K. (1991). Portfolios: Solution to a problem. In P. Belanoff & M. Dickson (Eds.), *Portfolios: Process and product* (pp. 165–173). Portsmouth, NH: Boynton/Cook.

Mills-Courts, K., & Amiran, M.R. (1991). Metacognition and the use of portfolios. In P. Belanoff & M. Dickson (Eds.), *Portfolios: Process and product* (pp. 101–112). Portsmouth, NH: Boynton/Cook.

Murphy, S. (1994a). Portfolios and curriculum reform: Patterns in practice. *Assessing Writing, 1,* 175–206.

Murphy, S. (1994b). Writing portfolios in K–12 schools: Implications for linguistically diverse students. In L. Black, D.A. Daiker, J. Sommers, & G. Stygall (Eds.), *New directions in portfolio assessment* (pp. 140–156). Portsmouth, NH: Boynton/Cook.

Murphy, S. (1997). Teachers and students: Reclaiming assessment via portfolios. In K. B. Yancey (Ed.), *Situating portfolios* (pp. 72–88). Logan: Utah State University Press.

Murphy, S., & Smith, M. A. (1992a). Looking into portfolios. In K.B. Yancey (Ed.), *Portfolios in the writing classroom* (pp. 49–60). Urbana, IL: National Council of Teachers of English.

Murphy, S., & Smith, M. A. (1992b). *Writing portfolios: A bridge from teaching to assessment.* Markham, Ontario: Pippin.

Naiman, N., Fröhlich, M., Stern, H., & Todesco, A. (1978). *The good language learner* (Research in Education Series, No. 7). Toronto: Ontario Institute for Studies in Education.

Navarrete, C. J. (1990). Reaching out: Using portfolios to combine formal and informal assessments. *EAC-West News, 4*(1), 8–9.

Nevo, N. (1989). Test-taking strategies on a multiple-choice test of reading comprehension. *Language Testing, 6*(2), 199–215.

North, B. (1991). Standardisation of continuous assessment grades. In J. C. Alderson & B. North (Eds.), *Language testing in the 1990s* (pp. 167–177). London: Modern English Publications/British Council, Macmillan.

North, B. (1993a). *The development of descriptors on scales of proficiency: Perspectives, problems, and a possible methodology*, Washington, DC: National Foreign Language Center.

North, B. (1993b). *Scales of language proficiency: A survey of some existing systems*. Strasbourg: Council of Europe.

North, B. (1994a). Itembanker: A testing tool for language teachers. *Language Testing Update, 6*, 85–97.

North, B. (1994b). *Perspectives on language proficiency and aspects of competence: A reference paper discussing issues in defining categories and levels*. Strasbourg: Council of Europe.

North, B. (1995): *The development of a common framework scale of descriptors of proficiency based on a theory of measurement*. Unpublished doctoral dissertation, Thames Valley University.

North, B. (in press). Perspectives on competence, proficiency and language as use. *Language Learning*.

Nunan, D. (1988) *The learner-centered curriculum*. London: Cambridge University Press.

Nyhus, S. E. (1994). *Attitudes of non-native speakers of English toward the use of verbal report to elicit their reading comprehension strategies*. Unpublished master's thesis, University of Minnesota, Minneapolis.

Olson, G. M., Duffy, S. A., & Mack, R. L. (1984). Thinking-out-loud as a method for studying real-time comprehension processes. In D.E. Kieras & M.A. Just (Eds.), *New methods in reading comprehension research* (pp. 253–286). Hillsdale, NJ: Lawrence Erlbaum Associates.

O'Malley, J. M., Chamot, A. U., Stewner-Manzanares, G., Kupper, L., & Russo, R. (1985). Learning strategies used by beginning and intermediate ESL students. *Language Learning, 35*(1), 21–46.

O'Malley, J. M., & Pierce, L. V. (1994). State assessment policies, practices, and language minority students. *Educational Assessment, 2*(3), 213–255.

O'Malley, J. M., & Pierce, L. V. (1996). *Authentic assessment for English language learners*. Boston: Addison-Wesley.

Oppenheim, A. N. (1992). *Questionnaire design, interviewing and attitude measurement*. London: Pinter Publishers.

Oskarsson, M. (1978). *Approaches to self-assessment in foreign language learning*. London: Pergamon.

Oskarsson, M. (1984). *Self-assessment of foreign language skills: A survey of research and development work*. Council for Cultural Cooperation, Strasbourg, France. (ERIC Document Reproduction Service No. ED 256 172).

Oxford, R., Nyikos, M., & Crookall, D. (1987). *Learning strategies of university foreign language students: A large-scale study*. Washington, DC: Center for Applied Linguistics.

Paulson, F. L., Paulson, P. R., & Meyer, C. A. (1991). What makes a portfolio a portfolio? *Educational Leadership, 48*(5), 60–63.

Perlman, C. (1994). *The CPS performance assessment idea book*. Chicago: Board of Education of the City of Chicago.

Pierce, B. M., Swain, M. & Hart, D. (1993). Self-assessment, French immersion, and locus of control. *Applied Linguistics, 14*, 25–42.

Pierce, L. V., & O'Malley, J. M. (1992). *Portfolio assessment for language minority students*. Washington, DC: National Clearinghouse for Bilingual Education.

Pollitt, A. (1991). Response to Alderson, bands and scores. In J. C. Alderson & B. North (Eds.), *Language testing in the 1990s* (pp. 87–94). London: Modern English Publications/British Council, Macmillan.

Porter, C., & Cleland, J. (1995). *The portfolio as a learning strategy.* Portsmouth, NH: Heinemann.

Pressley, M., & Afflerbach, P. (1995). *Verbal protocols of reading: The nature of constructively responsive reading.* Mahwah, NJ: Lawrence Erlbaum Associates.

Privette, L. M. (1993). The empty space. In K. Gill (Ed.), *Process and portfolios in writing instruction* (pp. 60–62). Urbana, IL: National Council of Teachers of English.

Radford, J. (1974). Reflections on introspection. *American Psychologist, 29*(4), 245–250.

Ramírez, A. G. (1986). Language learning strategies used by adolescents studying French in New York schools. *Foreign Language Annals, 19*(2), 131–141.

Reynolds, N. (1994). Graduate writers and portfolios: Issues of professionalism, authority, and resistance. In L. Black, D.A. Daiker, J. Sommers, & G. Stygall (Eds.), *New directions in portfolio assessment* (pp. 201–209). Portsmouth, NH: Boynton/Cook.

Robinson, M. (1991). Introspective methodology in interlanguage pragmatics research. In G. Kasper (Ed.), *Pragmatics of Japanese as native and target language* (pp. 29–84). (Tech. Rept. No. 3). Honolulu: Second Language Teaching and Curriculum Center, University of Hawaii.

Romano, T. (1994). Removing the blindfold: Portfolios in fiction writing classes. In L. Black, D.A. Daiker, J. Sommers, & G. Stygall (Eds.), *New directions in portfolio assessment* (pp. 73–82). Portsmouth, NH: Boynton/Cook.

Sajavaara, K. (1987). Second language production: Factors affecting fluency. In H. Dechert & M. Raupach (Eds.), *Psycholinguistics models of production* (pp. 45–65). Norwood, NJ: Ablex.

Schärer, R. (1992). A European language portfolio—A possible format. In R. Schärer & B. North, *Towards a common European framework for reporting language competency.* Washington, DC: National Foreign Language Center.

Schegloff, E. (1987). Between macro and micro: Contexts and other connections. In J. Alexander, B. Giessen., R. Munch, & N. Smelser (Eds.), *The micro-macro link.* Berkeley: University of California Press.

Schneider, G., North, B., & Richterich, R. (in press). *Evaluation et auto-évaluation de la compétence en langues étrangères aux points d'intersection du systeme d'enseignement suisse.* Zürich: National Science Research Council.

Schneider, G., & Richterich, R. (1992). Transparency and coherence: Why and for whom? In *Transparency and coherence in language learning in Europe: Objectives, assessment and certification* (pp. 43–49). Strasbourg: Council of Europe.

Segal, K. W. (1986). *Does a standardized reading comprehension test predict textbook prose reading proficiency of a linguistically heterogenous college population?* Unpublished doctoral dissertation, University of Texas, Austin.

Seldin, P. (1991). *The teaching portfolio.* Bolton, MA: Anker.

Seliger, H. W. (1983). The language learner as linguist: Of metaphors and realities. *Applied Linguistics, 4*(3), 179–191.

Shrauger, J. S., & Osberg, T. M. (1981). The relative accuracy of self-predictions and judgments by others in psychological assessments. *Psychological Bulletin, 90*, 322–351.

Skehan, P. (1984). Issues in the testing of English for specific purposes. *Language Testing, 1*, 202–220.

Smagorinsky, P. (1998). Thinking and speech and protocol analysis. *Mind, Culture, and Activity, 5*(3), 157–177.

Smith, C. A. (1991). Writing without testing. In P. Belanoff & M. Dickson (Eds.), *Portfolios: Process and product* (pp. 279–291). Portsmouth, NH: Boynton/Cook.

Smith, M. A. (1993). Introduction: Portfolio classrooms. In M.A. Smith & M. Ylvisaker (Eds.), *Teachers' voices: Portfolios in the classroom* (pp. 1–9). Berkeley, CA: National Writing Project.

Smith, M.A., & Ylvisaker, M. (Eds.). (1993). *Teachers' voices: Portfolios in the classroom.* Berkeley, CA: National Writing Project.

Smith, P. C., & Kendall, J. M. (1963). Retranslation of expectations: An approach to the construction of unambiguous anchors for rating scales. *Journal of Applied Psychology, 47*, 2.

Sommers, J. (1991). Bringing practice in line with theory: Using portfolio grading in the composition classroom. In P. Belanoff & M. Dickson (Eds.), *Portfolios: Process and product* (pp. 153–164). Portsmouth, NH: Boynton/Cook.

Sommers, J. (1997). Portfolios in literature courses: A case study. *Teaching English in the Two Year College, 24*, 220–234.

Spolsky, B. (1986). A multiple choice for language testers. *Language Testing, 3*, 147–158.

Spolsky, B. (1993). Testing and examinations in a national foreign language policy. In K. Sajavaara, S. Takala, D. Lambert, & C. Morfit (Eds), *National foreign language policies: Practices and prospects* (pp. 194–214). Institute for Education Research: University of Jyvaskyla.

Stratman, J. F., & Hamp-Lyons, L. (1994). Reactivity in concurrent think-aloud protocols. In P. Smagorinsky (Ed.), *Speaking about writing: Reflections on research methodology* (pp. 89–112). Thousand Oaks, CA: Sage.

Sunstein, B. S. (1992). Staying on course: One superintendent. In S. H. Graves & B. S. Sunstein (Eds.), *Portfolio portraits* (pp. 129–145). Portsmouth, NH: Heinemann.

Swanson-Owens, D., & Newell, G. E. (1994). Using intervention protocols to study the effects of instructional scaffolding on writing and learning. In P. Smagorinsky (Ed.), *Speaking about writing: Reflections on research methodology* (pp. 141–162). Thousand Oaks, CA: Sage.

Teaching English as a Second Language (TESOL). (1998). *Managing the assessment process: Guidelines for measuring the attainment of ESL standards.* Alexandria, VA: TESOL.

Thurstone, L. L. (1982). Attitudes can be measured. In B. D. Wright & G. Masters, *Rating scale analysis: Rasch measurement* (pp. 10–15). Chicago: Mesa Press.

Tierney, R. J., Carter, M. A., & Desai, L. E. (1991). *Portfolio assessment in the reading-writing classroom.* Norwood, MA: Christopher-Gordon.

Trim, J. L. (1978). *Some possible lines of development of an overall structure for a European unit/credit scheme for foreign language learning by adults.* Strasbourg: Council of Europe.

Trim, J. L. (1992). The background to the symposium: General orientation note. In *Transparency and coherence in language learning in Europe: Objectives, assessment and certification* (pp. 3–11). Strasbourg: Council of Europe.

Upshur, J. (1975). Objective evaluation of oral proficiency in the ESOL classroom. In L. Palmer & B. Spolsky (Eds.), *Papers on language 1967–1974.* Washington, DC: TESOL.

Upton, T. A. (1993). *An examination of the influence of ESL reading proficiency on recall protocols of Japanese students.* Unpublished doctoral dissertation, University of Minnesota, Minneapolis.

Van Ek, J. A. (1986). Objectives for foreign language teaching. *Scope, 1*, Council of Europe.

Van Hest, E. (1996). *Self-repair in L1 and L2 production: Studies in multilingualism* (Vol. 4) Tilburg: Tilburg University Press.

Van Hest, E., Poulisse, N., & Bongaerts T. (1997). Self-repair in L1 and L2 production: An overview. *ITL*, 85–117.

Verhoeven, L. (1989). Monitoring in children's second language speech. *Second Language Research, 5*, 141–155.

Wauters, J. K. (1991). Evaluation for empowerment: A portfolio proposal for Alaska. In P. Belanoff & M. Dickson (Eds.), *Portfolios: Process and product* (pp. 57–68). Portsmouth, NH: Boynton/Cook.

Weiser, I. (1994). Portfolios and the new teacher of writing. In L. Black, D. A. Daiker, J. Sommers, & G. Stygall (Eds.), *New directions in portfolio assessment* (pp. 219–229). Portsmouth, NH: Boynton/Cook.

Wenden, A. L. (1985). Learner strategies. *TESOL Newsletter, 19*(5), 1–7.

Wesche, M. (1993, August). *A comparative study of four placement instruments.* Paper presented at the 15th Language Testing Research Colloquium, Cambridge, England, and Arnhem, The Netherlands. (Eric Document Reproduction Service No. ED 364 064)

White, E. M. (1994a). Portfolios as an assessment concept. In L. Black, D. A. Daiker, J. Sommers, & G. Stygall (Eds.), *New directions in portfolio assessment* (pp. 93–102). Portsmouth, NH: Boynton/Cook..

White, E. M. (1994b). *Teaching and assessing writing* (2nd ed.). San Francisco, CA: Jossey-Bass.

Wiese, R. (1982). *Psycholinguistische Aspekte der Sprachproduktion: Sprechverhalten und Verbalisierungsprozesse.* Unpublished doctoral dissertation, Universität Bielefeld, Düsseldorf.

Wiese, R. (1984). Language production in foreign and native languages: Same or different? In H. Dechert, D. Möhle, & M. Raupach (Eds.), *Second language productions.* Tübingen: Gunter Narr Verlag.

Wolf, D. P. (1988). Opening up assessment. *Educational Leadership, 45*(1), 24–29.

Wolf, D. P. (1989). Portfolio assessment: Sampling student work. *Educational Leadership, 46*(7), 35–40.

Woods, A., & Baker, R. (1985). Item response theory. *Language Testing, 2.*

Wright, B. D., & Grosse, M. (1993). How to set standards: Rasch measurement. *Transactions of the Rasch measurement special interest group of the American Educational Research Association, 7*, 315–316.

Wright, B. D., & Linacre, J. J. (1987). Research notes: Rasch measurement. *Transactions of the Rasch measurement special interest group of the American Educational Research Association, 1*, 2–3.

Wright, B. D., & Masters, R. (1982) *Rating scale analysis: Rasch measurement.* Chicago: Mesa Press.

Wright, B. D., & Stone, M. H. (1979). *Best test design*, Chicago: Mesa Press.

Yagelski, R. P. (1997). Portfolios as a way to encourage reflective practice among preservice English teachers. In K. B. Yancey (Ed.), *Situating portfolios* (pp. 225–243). Logan: Utah State University Press.

Yancey, K. B. (Ed.). (1992a). Portfolios in the writing classroom. Urbana, IL: National Council of Teachers of English.

Yancey, K. B. (1992b). Teachers' stories: Notes toward a portfolio pedagogy. In K. B. Yancey (Ed.), *Situating portfolios* (pp. 214–222). Logan: Utah State University Press.

Author Index

Subject Index

Contributors

Glayol Ekbatani
Institute of ESL
St. John's University
Jamaica, NY 11439

Herbert Pierson
Institute of ESL
St. John's University
Jamaica, NY 11439

Andrew D. Cohen
University of Minnesota
ILASLL, 320 16th Avenue S.E.
Minneapolis, MN 55455

Margo Gottlieb
Illinois Resource Center
1855 Mt. Prospect Road
Des Plaines, IL 60018

Erna van Hest
National Institute for Educational
  Research
6801 MG Arnhem
The Netherlands

Alan Hirvela
ESL Composition Program
Ohio State University
Columbus, OH 43210-1285

Brian North
Eurocentres Foundation
Seestr. 247
CH-8038, Zürich
Switzerland

Diane Strong-Krause
Department of Linguistics
Brigham Young University
Provo, UT 84602